HARMUNY
WITHIN
DIVERSITY

A collection of papers delivered
at the International Haiku Conference
in St Albans, UK
31 May - 2 June 2019

The British Haiku
Society

Founded 1990

Editors: Colin Blundell with Iliyana Stoyanova and David Bingham, IHC Organising Committee

Cover: 'Japanese Quince' - Watercolour by Elisaveta Ilieva; Graphic design by Sider Evtimov (SeeDesign Ltd)

ISBN: 978-1-906333-12-6

Published by:
The British Haiku Society
79 Westbury Rd
Barking
Essex IG11 7PL
website: http://britishhaikusociety.org.uk/

Printed by:
Direct Services Ltd
www.directservices.bg
Todor Todorov
gsm: +359 886 101016
This book is printed on Xerox iGEN platform –
for more information please visit www.xerox.com

CONTENTS

Introduction

The British Haiku Society was the sponsor and organiser of an International Haiku Conference which took place in the historic city of St Albans, UK on the weekend of Friday, 31st May to Sunday, 2nd June 2019.

The overall theme of the conference was 'Haiku Crossing Cultures: Harmony within Diversity'. Along with the UK participants, people travelled from Europe, including Bulgaria, France, Germany, Italy, Poland, Sweden and Switzerland, and from Japan and the USA to attend this exciting event.

Over three days the conference programme offered a variety of presentations, performances, workshops, visits to local attractions, as well as a ginko and a haiku contest. The participants had the opportunity not only to meet old friends but also to form new relationships along the way and create some special memories.

The feedback from the conference was very positive and so The British Haiku Society decided to produce this volume which contains all the papers which were presented.

We would like to thank the speakers who kindly provided their materials for publication and who made the conference experience a truly unforgettable one.

We hope you find the work in this book as interesting and stimulating as the conference participants did and we hope to see you at future BHS events.

Iliyana Stoyanova and David Bingham
(International Haiku Conference Organising Committee)

Haiku Crossing Cultures, Harmony within Diversity

British Haiku Society President's Opening Remarks

In his opening speech, Colin Blundell welcomed members from Japan & America & Sweden & Poland, Bulgaria, Wales, London, Shropshire & Yorkshire and so on... to a country that had so far resisted being de-internationalised by Farage &Co.

He thanked Iliyana Stoyanova & David Bingham & and others who had been quietly working away behind the scenes to gather us all together. He continued, with his tongue in his cheek, at least to begin with, in the following way...

I'm not quite sure why I stand before you as President. Some people who choose to label themselves 'President' seem to imagine that they have a sort of divine right to the role, dropping bombs whenever & wherever they like. My own model would be ex-President José Mujica of Uruguay who spurned the Presidential Palace to live on his wife's farm and gave much of his income away to those who needed the cash. That seems to me to be an appropriately humble frame of mind for a haiku-writer

'President' certainly feels a strange label for one who has for a very long time labelled himself 'Tolstoyan anarchist'. I suppose it's just because I've been around so long in *The British Haiku Society* that, like an old dilapidated bit of seaweed, I've at last risen to the surface of the sea.

New members of BHS used to be assigned a number. I joined up not long after Numbers 1, 2 & 3 had started things off. I was made Number 23 after sending this dreadful hycoo to David Cobb (Number 2) on 26th September 1990:-

> I've always wanted
> to join a haiku club but...
> Japan's so far off

James Kirkup was number 1. I certainly do feel rather pleased to be stepping into a space previously occupied by this fellow anarchist who became a personal much-loved friend. I stopped the numbering practice which was becoming a bit unwieldy when I was Membership Secretary in the late 90's. Had we continued to turn people into numbers the latest member would no doubt be around 10,000. Many have come and gone but some of us have persisted. I always think of Frank Williams, ace photographer & haiku-writer, as 'Number 439' from 1996. People aren't numbers, though the way we use language often makes us think they are.

How did the BHS start? Well, it's always been 'international' or 'cross-cultural', from a section in *Blithe Spirit* called *The Pathway* (for other than 'British' haiku) beginning in October 1992 to David Cobb's publication *Euro-haiku* (2007) and beyond In fact BHS literally began in truly international space. David Cobb, who started it all off, writes in his introduction to the *Red Moon Press* anthology *Anchorage* (2014):-

My way into haiku started in total darkness over [Anchorage] Alaska [on the 7th day of the 7th month of 1977]. I was half a flight away from Japan on my maiden trip [to organise English Language Teaching material (?)]. Flipping idly through the in-flight magazine, I paused to read, 'Why not write haiku?' The feuilleton spelled out simple rules and I would surely have ample leisure during my ten-week stay. So why not? Perhaps my new Japanese friends might receive them as compliments. As we came in to land at Anchorage I observed a glacial river below our wings and rendered it into seventeen syllables.

The resulting haiku is not recorded in David's book but his way of perceiving may have been transformed later into

30,000 feet –
for a minute the Ganges
bearing sins away

David came across James Hackett; Mokuo Nagayama in Japan suggested David start a British group. For a contact, HSA suggested Dee Evetts who happened to be visiting UK to see his mum. Together they set up what was known as a 'Haiku Interest Group' – which is where I came in. David was the brains behind *The Consensus*, a provisional definition of haiku, which was eventually adopted by poetry groups in New Zealand, Romania and Croatia. Cor Van den Heuvel wrote to David to say that the BHS *Consensus* was the best description of the parameters of haiku he had ever seen. Renamed 'English Haiku: a Composite View', it still heads up our Members' Handbook.

I had a reply from David and a long friendship began. At 93 he's somewhat weak on his pins and has had cataract operations this month. I present you all with a little book celebrating a long friendship. What we called the first volume of *Blithe Spirit* (title suggested by James Kirkup – it was a play on 'Blyth' and the description of the lark in Shelley's poem) opened with my first proper editorial thus:-

> BHS Committee members meet in the sort of places where haiku/senryu simply ooze out of the woodwork – a pub in darkest Hampstead, an Italian restaurant, London railway termini eating places and windy corners here and there. Usually it is impossible to hear what anybody else is saying: this preserves the mental discipline necessary for the production of pithy little poems; it was in just such circumstances that David Cobb handed us a bulging orange folder. I thought he said, "Would you like another piece of pizza?" but what he actually said was, so it turns out, "You're now in charge of the BHS Journal!"

I had come across the idea of haiku around 1963 when I first read Alan Watts' *The Way of Zen*: the last chapter on 'Zen in the Arts' changed the way I think of making anything at all of an arty-crafty nature. It was nothing complicated: Western thinkers work on the assumption that the thinker has something to think about; in Zen, thinker and thing-thought are one; if you write about a tree, first become the tree, about a landscape first become the landscape. Doer and Deed are one. Seeking is finding and finding is seeking.

Like you, I expect, I've been amusing myself by imagining something of what we might be expecting in the next couple of days so that it will not be too much of a daze.

David Lanoue starts his book on Issa (*Pure Land Haiku*) with

> locked in a staring contest
> me...
> and a frog

which always makes me think of myself at 3/4 years of age bending down tracking newts in my father's rock-garden with the idea that was very clear to me then that the rockery was the entire universe which I take to be the way haiku works – in my small universe I became a newt. I'm looking forward to his piece on *Gendai Issa* – I imagine, for modern times, aspects of modernity in Issa, or, perhaps, a look at haiku that could have been written yesterday. David has written '...we do best by Issa if we open ourselves to each haiku with the same non-grasping attention we might pay to a bird warbling in a tree...'

Tracing Zen-think in Western thinkers & writers, RHBlyth quotes Thoreau – 'Human beings are trees walking; trees are human beings that can't walk...' Had Wordsworth been into haiku, even wandering lonely like a cloud, he could have saved a lot of ink:-

> all these daffodils!
> beside a lake
> fluttering

A different way of thinking, not comparing one thing with another, not engaging in poetic excesses, not going overboard with words, not from a personal point of view, I-less in the Lake District (rather than Gaza). What would it be like if, as in some languages, posing a problem for a translator, we had no word for 'I'? Doing Latin at school. It didn't occur to me all those years ago that *amo* has no pronoun. It's not 'I love' but 'there is a loving for me'... This perhaps has some relevance both to the way people in different cultures think about haiku and to what **Judy Kendall** calls a *Whirlpool of Translation.*

I take it that the original human brain is something we all have in common; it works in the same way for all of us; it sees/hears/feels in the same kind of way; it's a UNITY. It's what we choose to do with the result of mental activity that causes DIVERSITY. All people are poets, said Keats; but we think in different ways as influenced by the language we have at our disposal.

Studying Native American languages in the 1920's, Benjamin Lee Whorf developed the idea that the language you have at your disposal actually creates the world in which you imagine you live. In which case it's probably true, as Blyth said that 'Nothing divides one so much as thought...' Both internally and across all our artificial borders.

As a very simple example, take the way the language of colour works. Most people here think of 'black' as 'death' but in China the colour 'white' stands for 'death'. White for us might symbolize purity – it's used for brides' dresses, but no Chinese woman would ever wear white to her wedding. Instead, she usually wears red, the colour of good luck. For us 'red' means 'warning'. Well...

We step into a different way of thinking – not observer/observed, but finding out what happens when you become the flutter of daffodils. Science Fiction Fantasy writers have always offered us the chance to step into other worlds and they give us an opportunity to place ourselves in what would have to be a different way of thinking. In *Blithe Spirit* January 1991 I reviewed a small pamphlet entitled *We are not Men* by Steve Sneyd which included

> under the hundred
> suns we wither: no starships
> come to pull our ploughs

Strikes me as a rather nice metaphor for our times. No magic starships come to pull us out of Brexit... And we wither under just one sun.

So I look forward to **Ralf Bröker:** *Scibun or What Kind of Haiku They Don't Read on Rigel IV?*

It's my belief that true haiku are conceived in space – the inner space of Nothingness that can be arrived at without thinking about it so that haiku arrive accidentally out of thin air.

We are in a time when Post-modernism – the forgetting of the past, abandonment of Grand Theories – and we are faced with the spectacle of 'anything goes' in haiku. In JUXTA 4/1, Clayton Beach, whoever he might be, writes:-

> ...there is no truly 'traditional' haiku in English, at least regarding Japanese tradition, and the original expositions of the form in English were riddled with [Blyth's] inaccuracies that distorted our ideas of that tradition. This knowledge liberates us to experiment with what haiku might mean in English, since we'll have to build

much of our own tradition from the ground up, but it also leaves the question of why we persist in calling our work 'haiku' in the first place, and continue to claim fidelity to the Japanese form...

I do not require Clayton Beach's minor fantasy to liberate myself; I believe, all human brains being constructed in the same way physically, that anybody can get themselves into Zen-mode. It's therefore exciting to have **Ikuyo Yoshimura:** (*RH Blyth and his influence in the modern haiku world: Relationship between Blyth and James W Hackett*) to remind us of the origins of the way we in the BHS conceive of haiku – in a Blithe kind of way. Hot off the press is a reprint of *The Genius of Haiku*, a compendium of extracts from Blyth, originally devised by David Cobb in 1994 @ £10 a go during the Conference.

In *The Genius of Haiku* pp 136-138 Blyth has this lovely vision of the future of haiku:-

The latest development in the history of haiku is one which nobody foresaw – the writing of haiku outside Japan, not in the Japanese language. We may now assert with some confidence that the day is coming when haiku will be written in Russia (though communistic haiku, like capitalistic or Christian or Buddhist or atheistic haiku, is a glorious impossibility), in the Celebes, in Sardinia. What a pleasing prospect, what an Earthly Paradise it will be, the Esquimaux blowing on their fingers as they write haiku about the sun that never sets or rises, the pygmies composing jungle haiku on the gorilla and the python, the nomads of the Sahara and Gobi deserts seeing a grain of sand in a world [a world in a grain of sand..]

Charles Trumbull presents: *Georgia O'Keeffe and the Haiku Aesthetic.* Close up flowers & distant mountains. To write a haiku, Shiki recommends: 'Look at the violet at your feet, then look up at the distant mountain!'

I met Charlie in Huntsville in March 1997 when we both attended a course on setting haiku to music. He has written hugely about haiku. In *Simply Haiku* Vol 2/5 2004, for instance, there's his one of many attempts down the years, including a BHS member David Platt's

6

computerised DNA finger-printing methods, to define the differing ways in which haiku-writers approach the subject: *12 ways of defining oneself in relation to haiku-writing.* Charlie left his 'Highly Technical Figure V' blank and so, responding to his challenge to indulge in a Mind Game, I've had the temerity to design a model which I hope fills in his black void. You might like to use some of your spare time this weekend doodling on the diagram and comparing your ID with ID's of others!

NOTE: *The model is shown on page 8. This was an offering of notes to go with it:-*

'Haiku' is what's known as a 'polymorphous concept' – it has no one meaning unless one subscribes to the simple-minded 'three lines, 5-7-5, observation of Nature' kind of definition.

In the article referred to at the top of my 'Semantic Differential Analysis' grid, Charles rather compellingly identifies twelve possible ways ('propositions') of thinking about the nature & function of haiku. The argument goes that every serious haiku writer, whether they know it or not, will sit conceptually somewhere in relation to each dimension between one extreme and the other. Where they sit will also affect their judgement about 'good' and 'bad' haiku.

Completion of the grid will bring home to each of us what our take on haiku is and comparisons will be sure to provoke discussion.

In 2003, Charles, rather whimsically, said his 'Haiku ID' was 2723-4542-4353; I was interested to discover that mine was 'currently' 0935-5725-6506 reading down the page. This reminded Charles that one's Haiku ID is not fixed in concrete for all time but, looking again at his article after 15 years a few months ago, he said he was interested to observe that he hadn't changed much but that I had clocked up some extremes which he hadn't – this is obvious from our comparative patterns.

As an example, my pattern of belief is depicted by the solid line, Charles' pattern by the dotted line. If he & I were to sit down and discuss our patterns in detail, interesting complex differences & similarities would emerge. This is not about rights & wrongs but about differences in the way we individually construct the nature of something that appears to be 'the same' because there's just one word to represent what we seem to be talking about. We variously mean different things – it's as well that we know this fairly clearly.

CHARLES TRUMBULL'S HAIKU TWELVE DIMENSIONAL SPACE (2003)

(*Simply Haiku: An E-Journal of Haiku and Related Forms* September-October 2004, vol. 2, no. 5)

Dimensions & propositions

Highly Technical Figure V 12 Dimensions Mind Game
A Semantic Differential Analysis

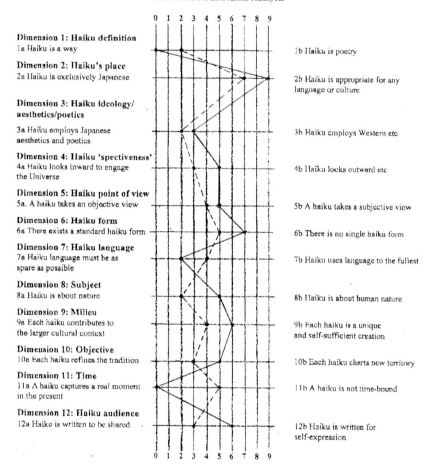

Dimension 1: Haiku definition
1a Haiku is a way — 1b Haiku is poetry

Dimension 2: Haiku's place
2a Haiku is exclusively Japanese — 2b Haiku is appropriate for any language or culture

Dimension 3: Haiku ideology/aesthetics/poetics
3a Haiku employs Japanese aesthetics and poetics — 3b Haiku employs Western etc

Dimension 4: Haiku 'spectiveness'
4a Haiku looks inward to engage the Universe — 4b Haiku looks outward etc

Dimension 5: Haiku point of view
5a. A haiku takes an objective view — 5b A haiku takes a subjective view

Dimension 6: Haiku form
6a There exists a standard haiku form — 6b There is no single haiku form

Dimension 7: Haiku language
7a Haiku language must be as spare as possible — 7b Haiku uses language to the fullest

Dimension 8: Subject
8a Haiku is about nature — 8b Haiku is about human nature

Dimension 9: Milieu
9a Each haiku contributes to the larger cultural context — 9b Each haiku is a unique and self-sufficient creation

Dimension 10: Objective
10a Each haiku refines the tradition — 10b Each haiku charts new territory

Dimension 11: Time
11a A haiku captures a real moment in the present — 11b A haiku is not time-bound

Dimension 12: Haiku audience
12a Haiku is written to be shared — 12b Haiku is written for self-expression

In 2003 Charles said that his Haiku ID was   2723-4542-4353
Colin Blundell's Haiku ID is currently   0935-5725-6506

(For a definition of 'Semantic differential' (Osgood 1969) see
methods.sagepub.com › encyclopedia-of-survey-research-methods)

8

And then we have **Antoaneta Nikolova and Yordan M. Georgiev** on *Nano-haiku.*

I had to look up Nano-haiku which, so it seems, combines poetry, visual art and advanced nanofabrication technologies to explore the interaction between the top-down Electron Beam Lithography and bottom-up Directed Self-Assembly of Block Co-Polymers in conjunction with the shortest poetic form, haiku to create self-organised nanopatterns... the samples were immersed in ethanol for 15 hours at 40° centigrade to dissolve the copolymer. In areas within and in-between the individual characters and syllables of the poems, unusual patterns were observed – hence, nanohaiga! Got it! I trust we shall get it...

The relationship between haiku mentality and other forms of human activity, music, art, proper poetry, novel-writing, chemistry is always fascinating. **Ian Storr** on *Haiku & Glass* will remind me of a Haiku & Glass project (2003/4) a few of us spent much rewarding time on.

Coming to haiku so relatively late in the day historically, it's amazing to realise how early last century it hit the West. The Imagists, Ezra Pound and many global mainstream writers of prose & poetry, often make us contemplate the difference between ordinary writing and haiku-writing... and then there's **Paul Chambers** on *Lorca.*

Cor van den Heuvel acknowledges the way his haiku-writing was influenced by the French novelist Robbe-Grillet who didn't write haiku as far as I know but whose prose is very haikuic. Here's a 'found haiku' that leapt out at me from the haikuic prose of one of his splendid novels:-

> I become no more
> than this fringe of stones
> bordering the waterline

And while I have been talking to you I have been no more than a bit of dilapidated old seaweed on this sea of faces in a hall of haiku... Let the games begin.

Colin threw his speech notes into the air and strode off...

9

HAIKU: THE WHIRLPOOLS OF TRANSLATION

Judy Kendall *(Reader in English and Creative Writing, University of Salford)*

Let's begin with a number of questions the answers to which should be quite revealing both about your approach to haiku and to translation.

Do you like to know if the haiku you are reading has been translated? If so consider why. Can you spot a translation if you've not been informed? What gives it away (an interesting phrase since this suggests translation is something to disguise or hide)? Does your reception of the haiku change when you realise it is a translation? Do you like to see the haiku in the original even if you cannot read it, and what are the reasons for this? What about hearing it? Do you like to have the literal as well as the literary translation to hand? If so, why? What do you gain?

I have an abiding interest in the process of translation of poetry, not just haiku, although my interest began with experience of co-translation of haiku. I also translate, or co-translate, old English riddles and poems and poetic prose from several European languages that I do not know – such as Frisian, Hungarian, Romanian, Russian. When I do this, I usually work with the poet concerned, or at the very least a native/fluent speaker, but not always. Most of my Old English riddle translations come about via a very close relationship with various dictionaries and previous translations.

And I like to share my fascination with language and the incredibly rich process of translation, as well as with, in particular, the rich depths of Japanese both spoken and more particularly written. Also, I am a strong believer in the influence that the language and writing has on poetic form and aesthetics. That means that a poem in one language has particular qualities that are directly related to the qualities of that language.

In relation to the translation of Japanese poetry (and in particular Japanese haiku), there is much to share about the wonderful multiple complex ambiguous mysterious process of translation that is involved, as it relates to haiku and to what the Japanese language offers a writer of haiku. Even if the reader doesn't know Japanese it is still possible to get a strong flavour of this language and of how it works in particular haiku. I know this from my own experience as a collaborative translator. I often

10

work in languages I don't know, or don't know very well, with either the original poet or a fluent or native speaker of that language. And part of the process of translating the poem is for me the very valuable side-effect as I get a kind of insider view of that language otherwise might take me years to acquire. Indeed, the translation of poetry provides not only a window into the original poem, but into the language and culture and literature in which that poem was written.

Makoto Ueda indicates this along pretty much the same lines in *Bashō and His Interpreters*, a book in which he aims to bridge the gap between cultures, making Japanese culture, language, past Japanese commentary on Bashō haiku and insights on haiku available to Western readers of Bashō. He writes:-

Probably those who have the greatest potential to contribute at present [to 'the huge accumulated mass of past commentary on Bashō's hokku'] are non-Japanese readers of Bashō's hokku, who have been reared in a radically different cultural tradition. In order for their comments to be valuable, however, they need to be thoroughly familiar with the Japanese language and culture […].The task would not be easy, but I believe it can be done.
(Makoto Ueda, *Bashō and His Interpreters*, page 9)

This is quite a radical position with which other Japanese writers and critics disagree, some even going so far as to say, like Hisao Kanaseki in 'Haiku and Modern American Poetry', East-West Review 3 (1967-68): pp223-41, that 'it is impossible to write haiku in a language other than Japanese' [p229], citing the poetical nature of the Japanese language, the literary associations of the kanji, the 'very special state of mind' haiku demands [p232], and cultural resonances of words and objects chosen. Kanaseki also talks about the poetic visual effects of the kanji that cannot be replicated in other languages.

What follows now should give you some experiential knowledge in making up your own mind about these pronouncements. To do this, first I will consider definitions of translation, then show specially com-missioned examples and comments by some translators, and comment on the qualities of Japanese writing in a way that should give you the necessary information to start a co-translation process of your own.

11

The trusty *Oxford English Dictionary* defines 'translation' variously. It is 'The action of converting from one language to another and related senses.' Or it is 'A version of a word, a work, etc., in a different language.' Or it is 'The expression or rendering of a thing in another medium or form; the conversion or adaptation of a thing to another system, context, or use.'

The phrase 'and related senses' in the first definition suggests translation doesn't just include the words, and the word 'a version' in the second definition tells us there can be more than one version. This is also true of the references to 'another medium or form... system, context, or use' in the third definition.

What these definitions all show is that translation is complex, complicated, rich and a never-ending, open-ended process – a process that some translators now try to present to their public as 'thick translation'. There is no time to go into this concept here although I think this description of the process of translation as 'thick' is very helpful in reminding us of its thick rich difficulties. However, here is some of what Theo Hermans has said about what could be called thick translation to help flesh out this term:-

> ...engulfed by footnotes, annotations, explication, digressions, abundance of detail, diligent exploration of the depth, patient but relentless probing of and swirling around, towering annotations underscoring both their own necessity and the hollowness of the pretense that one linear text could adequately match another...
> (Theo Hermans: *Cross-Cultural Studies as Thick Translation*)

From these words, the ones most immediately applicable to our current enquiry are the descriptions of translation as 'a patient but relentless probing of and swirling around,' and 'the hollowness of the pretense that one linear text could adequately match another'.

To investigate further I have specially commissioned a number of translations of haiku from a variety of bilingual (or multi-lingual) translators, those who know haiku and those who do not. I sent them previously published haiku from Iliyana Stoyanova and Dave Bingham and allowed them to choose which, and how many, to translate. These

12

languages are Italian, German, Hausa and Pidgin. I asked the translators for comments on the process, including areas where they feel it did not work. This is obviously not a sufficient number to provide a proper statistical analysis but I hope that by looking at these few examples we will learn a little more about the process of translation, and will also inhabit the haiku themselves a little more – since translation is perhaps the closest kind of reading that can be done. We will also learn a little more about the differences of the qualities of the various languages.

The first translator, Lucia Nigri, is a highly talented English literature academic with special interests in drama and Shakespeare. She is Italian and has very good English.

In her translations, she took the old-fashioned route of working with syllables, which perhaps tells us something about Italian. She identified (in brackets) the number of syllables per line, and notes that in Italian the count of syllables is different than in English.

She translated Stoyanova's 'wild strawberries':-

> wild strawberries
> dad only remembers
> the match score
> (Iliyana Stoyanova, *Presence* 61 p 37)

twice like this:-

Fragole di bosco (6)	Fragole di bosco (6)
E papà che ricorda solo (9)	Il punteggio (4)
il punteggio (4)	Nel ricordo di papà (7)

Her notes on the process are as follows:-

The first version has a more dramatic/abrupt change from the memories of strawberries to the father. The conjunction 'e/and' signals that change of subject (from the poetic subject's memory to the dad's). This version works with the emotional distance between the subject and their father.

13

The second version has an 'affective quality' – it is sadder. The change of subject ('papà/dad' in Version 1 and 'punteggio/match score' in Version 2) highlights how Version 1 is loaded with a feeling of possible resentment, which is absent from the second version.

The second haiku she translated was also one of Stoyanova's. This was a haiku that I expected translators to have problems with – because of the loaded meaning of 'attached' in English which I thought might not translate well. Lucia proved me wrong, as far as Italian is concerned.

> attached
> to the rest of the world
> baby's first smile
> > (Iliyana Stoyanova, *Presence* 60 p 77)

> Ancorato (4)
> al resto del mondo (6)
> il sorriso del bambino (8)

Nigri notes that 'This was somehow easier to translate because there was less tension to be handled in the translation. Even syllables were easier to respect.'

The second translator, Alaric Searle, is not a writer or translator of haiku. He is a professor of military history and is not a poet. He is English, with very good German, and with strong links with China, where he was working when he got my email, to which he responded thus:-

> Many apologies for the lateness of my response. Your e-mail caught me at a bad moment – I had a workshop I was organising, the keynote came to stay for the weekend, then I was off to China. I am still here, but more or less done with business. I have had, though, internet connection problems in my hotel. When it rains it pours. Anyway...

Here are two of the Bingham haiku he translated – 'magpies' and 'tide ebbing':-

14

magpies
hidden in meadow grass
two for joy
> (D Bingham, *Presence*)

Elster, Elster
versteckt im Gras auf der Wiese
die zwei bedeuten einfach Freude

and

tide ebbing
in memory of Mum
written on a grey pebble
> (D Bingham, *Presence*)

Ebbe und Flut, Ebbe und Flut
In Erinnerung an Mutti.
Auf einem grauen Kieselstein geschrieben...

Searle notes that

> I don't know if my translations are particularly good. But the main problem is that German is heavily dependent upon punctuation. It is not a language which flows, but is quite heavy and staccato, if that makes sense. The only way in some cases where I thought I could achieve a poetic effect was through repetition. I also found that full-stops and other punctuation was necessary to achieve the right effect. I am not sure whether modern German poets feel they are able to dispense with punctuation in the way it is possible in English.

> I think there are fairly set forms for German poetry, so they might struggle a bit with this Japanese form.

Although it is clear from this that Searle is not a haiku poet, he still demonstrates a very strong awareness of specific qualities of the language into which he translated – which supports one of the points that this article is making. What is most interesting here is his comment on the quality of German as heavy and staccato rather than flowing, and his recourse in response to this to a use of repetition, with 'Elster, Elster', as Ralf Bröker, a German-speaking member of the Conference put it, sounding like a children's song – beautiful repetitions of sound that cannot be replicated in English.

The third translator, Vashti Suwa Gbolagun, is a PhD student in creative writing, fluent in English, Hausa and Nigerian Pidgin. She offered what she terms 'direct translations' and 'nuanced translations' 'implied translations' 'literal translations'. This alone immediately indicates to us her awareness of the differences of different kinds of translation processes – even if we are not yet exactly sure what she means by each.

She chose to attempt Stoyanova's 'wild strawberries':-

> wild strawberries
> dad only remembers
> the match score

In Pidgin English this becomes:-

> oyinbo fruit wey dey grow for bush
> naim papa remember
> wetin dem play for mach

> Hausa:-

> bambaron daji
> amma abin da baba ya tuna
> shine nawa aka sha kwalo

Of the Pidgin, she wrote that '...the direct translation does not convey the intended meaning in the original poem. It makes incoherent sense instead...' and of the Hausa she wrote that '...we do not have words for strawberry as it is not an indigenous fruit, so it was a bit challenging. I had to imply its meaning'...

She also tackled Bingham's 'tide ebbing':-

tide ebbing
in memory of Mum
written on a grey pebble

Pidgin:-

river wey dey finish
take remember mama
dem write am for stone

She noted that '...it was difficult to get a word for 'tide ebbing' in Pidgin, so I referred to river instead', and also that

In Hausa, it was too difficult to interpret this poem as words like 'tide ebbing', and 'grey pebble' as used to make sense in the original poem will not make sense if I translate them directly.'

It was easier to translate into Hausa than Pidgin as some of the words are not words that are familiar to the Pidgin language. However, in Hausa the interpretation of the words is what I used, while for Pidgin the implied meaning was used sometimes.

All these examples show quite clearly the awareness of translators of the differences between languages – and between them they cover several. If we now narrow this down to translation of haiku from Japanese to English we can see even more clearly how difficult and indeed impossible it is to recreate all the effects of one language in another. In the case of Japanese-English translation this is also true of the writing itself. It is not possible to recreate all the effects of Japanese writing in English since we do not have the depth in our letters that resides in the kanji.

This pertains to both prose and poetry. We can see one translator's feelings on this in Koun Franz' 'Translator's Note' to a translation of an essay by Kaneko Tohta from Japanese to English:

It is in the nature of ideograms that just one character almost always carries with it multiple nuances, if not a host of entirely different meanings. Often, context clarifies the direction of a

17

given character's meaning, but not always. And even then, because the Japanese reader knows the other potential nuances available, we can say that those nuances are present in that reader's experience of the word, even if it is understood that they are not primary.

('Poetic Language in Translation' Translator's Note by Koun Franz Kaneko TOHTA *Haiku as Life: A Kaneko Tohta Omnibus:Essays, an Interview, Commentary and Selected Haikuin Translation* Red Moon Press, p.63)

In many cases a single kanji or a single compound kanji includes many pictorial, aural and associative links – a multi-layered montage.

Take the kanji for 'leaf'. It is made up of visual references to grass, generations, trees. If we combine it with 'wind' to form the wonderful concept of 'the wind passing through the leaves, *hakaze*, 葉風′, 葉風 – we are adding to this complex understanding of leaf, as the three outward lines in the second kanji indicating a gust of wind blowing outwards, enclose what can exist as a separate kanji in its own right 虫 or insect, *mushi*. Thus, 'wind passing through the leaves', is made up of, or holds the seeds within it of grass+generation+tree and wind+insect.

To read English (in what is called the Latin alphabet) we skirt along the surface of the letters. We skim. This is most evident when reading joined-up handwriting. Each letter seems to lean into, or join onto, the next. We read along, we are pushed along, the line. B+A+T spells BAT, and thus a word is formed. It is as if we are viewing the letters from the side as they file by, one after the next.

This is very different from reading Japanese. Paul Claudel has explained this well: 'the Chinese letter faces you, the Latin letter shows its profile' (Tim Ingold, *Lines: A Brief History* p.134, cited in Billeter 1990:28 (*The Chinese Art of Writing* NY Rizzoli trans J.-M.Clarke and M. Taylor). Kanji (which are the Chinese letters he talks about) are observed face on. While the Latin alphabet, in which we write English, walks by us – or we walk by it – reading Japanese requires us to go *in* to the kanji.

We have already heard from Hisao Kanaseki – the writer who thinks haiku can only be written in Japanese. He stresses the importance of the ideogram or kanji in haiku. Any other language, and Kanaseki is really thinking of English here, would lack the poetic visual effects of the kanji. Among the crucial contributions kanji make to a poem are the combination and order of brushstrokes of which each kanji consists, and even the choice of tools, brush or pen, quality and thickness of paper, with which these strokes are executed and displayed. In other words, Kanaseki is referring to the *shodou* or the way of writing, in which beauty of the calligraphy of a poem, and the actual selection of particular kanji in it are crucial elements that contribute to the effect of the haiku.

A counter argument to the contribution of kanji and written characters to the effects of a poem crops up again and again from the early twentieth century to today. It was raised by David Lanoue in the 2019 International Haiku Conference. Do fluent native readers of Japanese kanji really see all the details that those of us who have studied kanji as adults do? Surely these elements just pass them by? This may be so, but may not always be so, as Lanoue himself admitted of at least one example of an Issa haiku. This reminds us of the ways in which readers can see more in haiku than the writer ever intended. Rather than invalidating the haiku, or the reader's reception of it, such surprising revelations seem often to confirm the value of that piece, which brings forth interpretations somehow latent, or hovering, between the words and the silent space, beyond it...

Perhaps the best answer to this particular issue resides in a short discussion of a haiku written by another participant in the Conference, Mariko Kitakubo. She wrote and then shared this with me shortly after I had presented much of the content of what is now in this article. She felt her haiku definitely made more poetic sense in Japanese than in English because of the visual contribution of the kanji she used. Her kanji for 'magpie' is made up of the elements of 'old' and 'bird', and the magpie, she tells me, is a bird that is disappearing in Japan, perhaps like the remains of the castle in the last line of the haiku. This works visually in the Japanese but not in the English. As she herself tells me, the English version, reproduced above the Japanese here, is less interesting. We miss that visual element:-

19

magpie
is singing a lullaby
castle ruins

鵲　kasasagi　(昔…long ago) (鳥…bird)

が　ga

守　mori

歌　uta

う　u

た　ta

ふ　u

城　siro

の　no

跡　ato

Having read so far, and with the inspiration of Kitakubo's response to this topic, you now have the necessary information and impetus, I hope, to start a co-translation process of your own. It requires work of course but is not beyond the capability of anyone who has read thus far.

Here are two haiku by Chiyo-ni, from Matto, very near where I used to live in Japan, followed in each case by much information. In each case I give you translations by Patricia Donegan and Yoshie Ishibashi from *Chiyo-Jo's Haiku Seasons*, the Japanese in romaji, a translated comment-

20

ary (but you should feel able to depart from this commentary), and the haiku in Japanese, as well as a literal translation, and some notes.

Chiyo-ni's haiku (1)

> spring
> stays
> in the iris

This is Donegan and Ishibashi's English translation.

In romaji, it reads:-

> yuku haru no
> o ya sonomama ni
> kakitsubata

(Note: In English, the *Iris ensata* is also known as Chiyo-no-haru, or as the Japanese Water Iris, Russian Iris, Japanese Flag Iris. Chiyo-no-haru means 'Chiyo's spring'.)

With it is an accompanying (translated) commentary – it's not clear who wrote this, or when:-

> Cherry blossoms are already scattered. In early summer, the blue flag iris which blooms beautiful deep purple flowers that look like wild iris. The end of spring, which is like the pattern at the end of a kimono cloth, is the thing that people long to keep. The blue flag iris, with a hint of purple colour, as of flying swallows, is blooming by the water. It connects the ending of the spring to the summer.

On the next page you will find the original kanji and hiragana which also have some furigana notes to aid the reading of the kanji. I have added further notes on the right in English.

行春（ゆくはる）の尾（お）やそのまゝ（ま）に杜若（かきつばた）

The first two kanji make up 'yuku haru': Yuku going/departing. Haru – spring. The next hiragana symbol 'no' equals ' 's' (the grammatical possessive). The fourth is the kanji 'o' – tail/end. So : 'departing spring's end'. The fifth is the hiragana symbol 'ya', a cutting word – it suggests a link like 'and' or a semi colon, but also gives a sense of suspension, like a dash or ellipsis...

For the next five symbols (if we include the 'ya'), the haiku continues to use simple flowing hiragana that spell out 'sonomama ni' – meaning 'as it is', 'just like that', 'let it be', 'left as it is'.

The last two symbols are very dense. They make up the compound kanji for 'kakitsubata' or iris. They evoke complex literary allusions (see the notes below). The kanji for 'kaki' carries the meaning 'woods/grove' and it is made up of the elements of 'tree' and 'earth/land'. The kanji for 'tsubata' carries the meaning of 'perhaps' or 'young'. In it we can see the radical which carries the meaning of 'grass' at the top, and under it the element that carries the meaning of 'stone' or 'pebble'.

The strong literary influences evoked by kakitsubata – Japanese iris:-

The Kakitsubata (カキツバタ、杜若), *Iris laevigata*) grows in the semi-wet land and is less popular, but is also cultivated extensively. It is a prefectural flower of Aichi Prefecture due to the famous tanka poem which is said to have been written in this area during the Heian period, as it appears in *The Tales of Ise* by Ariwara no Narihira (note that the beginning syllables are 'ka-ki-tsu-ha (ba)-ta').

Original text	Pronunciation	Meaning
から衣 きつゝなれにし つましあれば はるばるきぬる たびをしぞ思	Karakoromo Kitsutsu narenishi Tsuma shi areba, Harubaru kinuru Tabi o shizo omou	I have come so far away on this trip this time and think of my wife that I left in Kyoto

Kakitsubata at Ōta Shrine, Kyoto, is a National Natural Treasure. It was already recorded in a *tanka* by Fujiwara Toshinari also in the Heian period:-

Original text	Pronunciation	Meaning
神山や大田の沢のか きつばた ふかきたのみは色に 見ゆらむ	Kamiyama ya ōta no sawa no kakitsubata Fukaki tanomi wa iro ni miyu ramu	Like the *kakitsubata* at Ōta Wetland, a God-sent heaven, my trust in you can be seen in the color of their flowers.

(adapted from http://www.primidi.com/japanese_iris/kakitsubata)

Chiyo-ni's haiku (2)

> full moon –
> keeping it in my eyes
> on a distant walk

This is Donegan and Ishibashi's English translation.

In romaji, it reads

> meigetsu ya
> me ni okinagara
> toariki

With it is an accompanying (translated) commentary:-

In the sky the harvest moon (August 15th in the lunar calendar) played beautifully. Chiyo-jo was following the moon on her journey. For a traveller like her, it goes without saying, that she was receiving Buddha's clear light into her heart and was feeling the joy of travelling freely.

Here are the original kanji and hiragana which also have some furigana notes to aid the reading of the kanji. I have added further notes on the right in English. This is a good haiku to consider if you want to think about the visual contributions that kanji bring to haiku in Japanese: in the

23

Japanese writing, we have a clump of kanji, some flowing hiragana and another kanji clump; each 'clump' has different qualities.

名月や眼に置なが ら遠歩行

The first two symbols are kanji. The first 'mei' carries the meaning of 'famous' 'wise'. The second 'getsu' carries the meaning of 'month/ moon'. Together they mean 'full moon'. The next is the hiragana symbol 'ya'. It can mean 'and' and also can work as a cutting word, suggesting a link like 'and' or a semi colon, but also gives a sense of suspension, like a dash or ellipsis.....

Next we have 'me' – a kanji meaning 'eye' or 'eyeball'. It is made up of the kanji for eye (目) and another kanji which alone carries the meaning of silver. Together they read 'eyeball' [eye + silver]. After this comes the hiragana 'ni' (in). And then the kanji 'oki', carrying the meaning of 'place', 'put', 'deposit', 'keep'). If you look closely at this verb, you'll see it includes the element for 'me' or 'eye' (目) two times over. The horizontal one at the top is known as a sideways eye. So, **lots of light and a number of eyes in the kanji of first 2 thirds of this haiku.**

The next three hiragana symbols 'na ga ra' spell out an ending to the verb 'oki' – giving the sense of doing one thing while also doing something else (keeping it in the eyes while going on a distant walk), and I think the flowing 'surface' hiragana in which they are written emphasises this too

The last three kanji form a clump – like the clump at the start – but **here the emphasis is not on light and eyes but on progress, road, walking, steps:** tō means 'far' or 'distant' and also includes an element carrying the meaning 'advancing/ walking/ road' aru(ku) means 'walk' or 'step' and includes the radical 'stop', so suggests movements that have stages, stops or steps

Once you have absorbed all this you will have enough information, working alone or in small groups, to come up with your own translations of one or both of the above. If you are serious about gaining some experiential awareness of translation you will wish to pause the reading of this article here while you go back and study the two Chiyo-ni haiku and attempt your own versions of them. If not, then read on now and simply admire others' attempts.

In the case of the Haiku Conference a large number of haiku translations, sometimes produced extremely rapidly, resulted. Most people chose to work alone but not all. A large number chose to leave their haiku translations anonymous, whether through lack of confidence, lack of interest, or a humble belief in the importance of reducing that sense of 'I', I cannot say.

Here is a brief resumé of these translations, also transcribed below by me (and perhaps sometimes wrongly since they were all written or even scribbled on post-it notes in hands that were not always clear, thus inadvertent extra translations of the translations might have resulted too). I was pleased to see some attempts in other languages – French and German, Polish and Swedish, showing an awareness of difference of language quality in translation – directly relevant to our theme. In the first group, the relative wordiness of many of the translations was noteworthy, given the daring scarcity of the Donegan and Ishibashi attempt. Some translation theorists talk about a common need to provide redundancy when translating, as if we need more words to provide some of the alternative nuances the original might have – this is what makes Donegan and Ishibashi's English translation so daring. Bröker's German attempt perhaps comes nearest to theirs – although now I am comparing translations and not originals of course.

In the translations below, 'sonomama ni' is translated in a number of different ways, mainly keeping to the simplicity of the original, from Anon's 'hanging on' to Shimield's ellipses to Lawson's 'dawdles' and an anonymous 'lingering', and even perhaps Storr's 'wood's edge'. All these choices bring their own suggestions and nuances with them too of course. But I think my favourite is Bob Moyer's simple, matter-of-fact version in which he uses the brilliant 'stuck' (and 'still here') to convey a certain kind of sonomama ni.

In terms of other aspects of this first group, Blundell's 'rooted' stands out as, I am assuming here, an attempt to include something of the earthiness suggested by kakitsubata. I also like the anonymous 'falls of iris' which suggests autumn and ending, even though I wonder if this word is just a misreading by me of the writer's hand. There isn't a reference to autumn in the original but it does nicely I feel.

Here are all the translations of 'yuku haru':-

yuku haru no
o ya sonomama ni
kakitsubata

spring
stays
in the iris
(Donegan and Ishibashi's English translation)

Conference 'Translations':-

hanging on
inside the iris
spring
      Anon

the tail end of spring ... purple iris
      Andrew Shimield

iris
rooted just so
in spite of spring's end
      Colin Blundell

le printemps s'estompe ...
une dernière étincele
de l'iris
      Valeria Borouch

good-bye spring
the iris
dawdles behind
      Sarah Lawson

Departing spring...
newly out at the wood's edge
blue flag iris
      Ian Storr

the remains of spring
in the early summer
iris
      Ikuyo, Asuka, David

Lenz
macht halt
im Augenstern

      Ralf Bröker

spring fading...
a last spark
in the iris

      Valeria Barouch

26

spring
translated
into .. iris
    Anon

waits
the iris
golden petals
    Anon

new life
in falls of iris
lingering
    Anon

varen
forblir
i irisen
    Anon (Swedish)

Varen
stannar upp
i irisen
    Anon (Swedish)

jeszcza
trochme wiosny –
wirysie
    Anon (Polish)

still here
stuck in the iris
spring
    Bob Moyer

Frühling
bleibt
in der Iris
    Ralf Bröker

In the second group of translations we begin to see some translators tackling the issue of translation of writing (and visuality) specifically, translating not just words but kanji. I like Mick Tupling's 'Coiled metal /and whalebone', not an exact translation, but definitely one that recognises the richness inherent in the original ideograms. A number of writers have responded to the notes on the repeated references to light and eyes, Roger Watson for one making clever use of a Scottish/English homonym: 'aye in ma ee'n'. Mark Gilbert makes use of Japanese writing directions, going for vertical progression in which each word takes us forward to the next line but at the end we are left with a reflection 'in/my/eye'. Very pleasing work, I think. In a similar, and yet completely different way, FRED's (I know who this is but will let him remain as simple FRED) 'It shines my eyes:' also lets us question both causality and direction – which way is the light moving, who is 'doing' the shining, etc.

27

meigetsu ya
me ni okinagara
toariki

full moon –
keeping it in my eyes
on a distant walk
Donegan and Ishibashi's English translation

Conference 'Translations':-

full moon
lighting
my long road
Mark Ritchie

harvest moon –
I keep it in sight
walking far
Ikuyo, Asuka, David

bricht moon
aye in ma ee'n
on a lang w'ak
Roger Watson

Vollmond –
halte ihn im Auge
auf einem langen Weg
Ralf Bröker

full moon
sunlight in my eyes
on the pathway
Tim H

harvest moon
lighting
on a long walk
MK

Coiled metal
and whalebone
in my eye
Mick Tupling

full moon
lighting
my long road
Anon

It shines my eyes:
walking so far:
the full moon
FRED

28

one
more
step
full
moon
reflected
in
my
eye

Mark Gilbert

harvest moon
I keep it in sight
walking far
                    Anon

fullmane
följer den med blicken   OR
pa langpromenaden
                    Anon

fullmane
ögonenföljer den
pa langpromenaden

I watch
the long path
in the full moon
        Kate B Hall

man in the moon
my eyes open wide
as I tread the path
        Anon

full moon
sunlight in my eyes
on my lifeway
        Tim H

The very high quality of many of these attempts and their extremely varied nature tell us perhaps more than this article itself can do of how rich, varied and thick, the translation process is, from one language, culture, idiom and writing system to another, and another, and another.

A Reconstruction by Colin Blundell from Ralf's Notes – with his approval...

In order to answer the question 'What is a Scibun?', Ralf first of all consulted the Internet. He found a reference to 'scibun' in a text dated 1842 – a Treasure Chest or Word Dictionary of Spoken Old High German, edited etymologically and grammatically by Dr EG Graff. [This last sentence is made up of what I take to be the most important words in the initial page of the text which I seem to have managed to translate with the help of Google... CB]

Sprachschatz

oder

Wörterbuch

der

althochdeutschen Sprache,

in welchem

nicht nur zur Aufstellung der ursprünglichen Form und Bedeutung der heutigen hochdeutschen Wörter und zur Erklärung der althochdeutschen Schriften alle aus den Zeiten vor dem 12ten Jahrhundert uns aufbewahrten hochdeutschen Wörter unmittelbar aus den handschriftlichen Quellen vollständig gesammelt, sondern auch durch Vergleichung des Althochdeutschen mit dem Indischen, Griechischen, Römischen, Litauischen, Altpreufsischen, Gothischen, Angelsächsischen, Altniederdeutschen, Altnordischen die schwesterliche Verwandtschaft dieser Sprachen, so wie die dem Hoch- und Niederdeutschen, dem Englischen, Holländischen, Dänischen, Schwedischen gemeinschaftlichen Wurzelwörter nachgewiesen sind.

etymologisch und grammatisch bearbeitet

* * *

Dr. E. G. Graff,

Königl. Preufs. Regierungsrathe und ordentlichem Mitglede der Königl. Akademie der Wissenschaften zu Berlin.

Sechster und letzter Theil.

Die mit S anlautenden Wörter.

Berlin,

beim Verfasser und in Commission der Nikolaischen Buchhandlung

---

1842.

In the body of the text there are three sub-headings under the label 'scibun': (1) 'speram' of which the Google translation is 'sperm'; (2) 'sphaerulas' which means 'small spheroids'; (3) 'scatulis' which is apparently something of a medical nature. It may therefore be supposed, perhaps, that the original meaning of 'scibun' was something to do with its being a pregnant phenomenon – so entirely relevant to our meaning.

But perhaps the word refers to some kind of wacky hairstyle of the kind some might wear on Rigel IV – a 'sci-bun'…

But what and where is Rigel IV? Another Internet search provides an answer of sorts:-

Rigel IV was the inhabited fourth planet of the Rigel system, less than ninety light years away from Earth. The planet was the homeworld to the Rigel IV natives, including the Hill People, and had deposits of boridium and murinite.

We are told that Humans began moving to Rigel IV after 2156. In 2266, the Redjac entity possessed Hengist, a native of Rigel IV, and killed several women [no doubt wearing sci-buns] on the planet. He was never caught and was only known as 'Beratis'. On Argelius II, Redjac committed a murder with a knife from Rigel IV's Argus River region.

In the 24th century, a brilliant astronomer with a fondness for the Betazoid Ambassador Lwaxana Troi resided on Rigel IV. He named a star after Lwaxana, or so she claimed, in 2367.

In mid-2370, Rigel IV hosted a nearly week-long conference on hydroponics attended by Keiko O'Brien.

According to *StarTrek.com*, Rigel IV was an M-class world. It was only ever mentioned in dialogue, that is, by hearsay.

It is perhaps not surprising that the chequered history of Rigel IV prevents us from having much in the way of evidence about the kind of haiku they don't read now in a place full of such excitements.

In actual fact, another story about Rigel is in existence: it was originally designated Beta Orionis, is apparently the seventh brightest star in the night sky and the brightest star in the constellation of Orion. Its brightness varies slightly, and it is occasionally outshone by Betelgeuse, itself a semi-regular variable star. Rigel looks blue-white to the naked eye, contrasting with orange-red Betelgeuse. Although appearing as a single star to the naked eye, Rigel is actually a multiple star system composed of at least four stars: Rigel A, Rigel Ba, Rigel Bb, and Rigel C.

Rigel is a massive blue supergiant calculated to be anywhere from 61,500 to 363,000 times as luminous as the Sun, whose radius it dwarfs over 70 times.

Such extreme intricacy constitutes the context in which haiku are both conceived and to be read, as Ralf now illustrates.

In view of her background, it is to be supposed that Linda Robeck [note the absence of sci-buns in her hair-style] would be more familiar with this last account since, having written poetry in various forms for as long as she could remember, after the Viking landing on Mars in 1976 inspired her to follow the stars, she took up a professionally qualified career in aerospace engineering. She worked successfully for NASA before retiring from the space business when she moved back home to New England with her husband. After that she worked part time from home as a technical writer and technical recruiter and returned to writing poetry and stories. She has appeared in *Frogpond*, *Modern Haiku*, *Mayfly*, *Acorn*, and so on.

seeking renewal –
the library's shelf
of self-help books

Linda Robeck's passion for space exploration merged with her writing: she has written Sci-bun.

What is a Sci-Bun, then, for real? In traditional Japanese poetry, the 'haibun' form often begins with a narrative that sets the stage and background for a haiku. A 'sci-bun' is therefore a narrative that winds its way somehow around a 'sci-ku'. These invented words derive from the category 'Science fiction' which is often called Sci-Fi, a sort of 'literature of ideas'. It typically deals with imaginative and futuristic concepts such as advanced science and technology, time travel, parallel universes, fictional worlds, space exploration, and extraterrestrial life. It often explores the potential consequences of scientific innovations. Isaac Asimov suggested that 'Science fiction can be defined as that branch of literature which deals with the reaction of human beings to changes in science and technology'.

From her vantage point outside aerospace engineering, a scibun seems the perfect way for Linda Robeck to merge space exploration and imaginative writing. Here are two of her scibun.

1

THE COLD DESERT

When the Space Shuttle first started to fly, it landed on a dry lake bed in the Mojave Desert of California. Back then they weren't sure if the brakes would stop it before it ran out of runway at Kennedy Space Center in Florida. At that time we were studying how the astronauts adapted to outer space, and we had to run our experiments on them as soon as they arrived, before they re-adapted to Earth. We set up our equipment in a hanger on the shore of the ancient lake and waited for the Shuttle to land. At night, the desert got very cold, and the snakes preferred the warmth lingering by our equipment. Every morning we looked under our desks before we sat down to check if a snake had curled up there in the night.

> shuttle landing
> rattlesnake
> beneath my desk

2

FIRE!

On the Mars Pathfinder mission, we had to be sure that we didn't send any Earth bacteria or spores on the spacecraft that might contaminate Mars. So each of us wore rubber gloves and head-to-toe clean room suits, and masks over our nose and mouth. The remarkably complicated little spacecraft had more explosives on it than any we had ever done before: explosives that opened latches, released the camera, sprung open the ramps, fired retro rockets, filled airbags, and freed the rover after its long journey. We armed the explosives by installing pyrotechnic devices, or 'pyros' as we called them, as the very last step before we closed it up for launch. By that time, with all of the rockets and fuel installed, our baby was a sizable bomb. The smallest spark at the wrong moment would set it off.

> installing pyros
> sweat
> inside my gloves

Ralf concluded his presentation with one of his own scibun. Linda Robeck's scibun are clearly related to her own professional experience; Ralf's haibun is a flight of fancy which nicely plays with the reader's perception.

Scibun 12

He had been rummaging around long enough in this rubble field. Now he turned to the excavation site, which had previously been worked through only by the assistants.

Casually – not to say listlessly – he poked with the carbon probe around in the ashes. Nothing. Of course, nothing. These creatures had destroyed all organic matter on their planet with their nuclear weapons, and in the millennia of contamination, the hot wind, acid rain and massive drops of temperature in winter time had weathered metal and concrete.

Only very rarely large bronze lumps were found, which might have been part of a raw material depot once. The barely visible characters on them had not yet been deciphered. Presumably they marked the type of material and their position in the storage.

A pretty crazy type from the Cryptology Department had put forward the weird thesis that it could represent names and numbers. However this was discarded by all recognised professionals, as these signs were more or less two dimensional and it was unimaginable to create complex techniques (that had obviously led to the death of this civilisation) with such limited writing.

He continued to poke around in the grey dust of the digging site, pushing aside small granite stabs that also bore these primitive signs. Often, a long longitudinal line occurred on them crossed with a short slash. Perhaps a primitive self-expression of the beings who once lived here? Or even a religious sign?

In any case that would support the hypothesis that those creatures here were not capable of developing nuclear weapons, and one of the many invasive structures of the universe had been raging here, What the hell...

He put aside the working stick, took a cartridge of *krpjg* out of the abdominal sac, stabbed his food tentacle into it and sucked the neon blue treat in seconds.

> the last human
> digs himself a last bed
> in that desert
> which we prepare for him
> even while asleep, asleep

GEORGIA O'KEEFFE AND THE HAIKU AESTHETIC
Charles Trumbull (with Lidia Rozmus)

Image 1: Georgia O'Keeffe

Note: This talk was originally presented at the Haiku North America conference in Santa Fe, New Mexico, in September 2017, a collaborative effort with sumi-e artist and haiku poet Lidia Rozmus. Lidia prepared the serious part, about Georgia O'Keeffe's exposure of Japanese aesthetics, while I combed through my Haiku Database to find verses that poets had written to or about paintings by O'Keeffe. For the presentation at the World Haiku Conference in St Albans, U.K., in June 2019, I shifted some of Lidia's words around, added some details about O'Keeffe's life and career, and included a few extra slides. The images used here are taken from various websites; source citations are provided at the end.

Georgia Totto O'Keeffe was born on a dairy farm near Sun Prairie, Wisconsin, in 1887. She showed an interest in art as early as grade school and pursued it in boarding schools in Wisconsin and Virginia. She studied briefly at the Art Students League in New York City and the Art Institute of Chicago, returning to the University of Virginia in Charlottesville. There in the summer of 1912 her teacher Alon Bement exposed her to the ideas of his mentor, Arthur Wesley Dow. This was O'Keeffe's first encounter with the Japanese aesthetic. She had aban-

37

doned art in her early twenties because it lacked meaning for her, but it was the influence of Dow that brought her back to painting.

Image 2. Arthur Wesley Dow

Arthur Wesley Dow (born 1857, Ipswich, Mass., died in 1922) was a painter, printmaker, photographer, and arts educator. He was inspired by the woodblock prints of Hokusai, and in 1892 he sought out Ernest Fenollosa, the influential curator of Japanese art at the Boston Museum of Fine Arts, who introduced Dow to the other masters of *sumi* ink painting and woodblock techniques. In 1893, Dow was appointed assistant curator at the Museum of Fine Arts under Fenellosa.

Image 3. *Circle* by Arthur Wesley Dow

Dow's approach emphasized harmonic composition, and was strongly influenced by Oriental art. He even advocated that his students practice using Oriental brushes and *sumi* ink in order to develop aesthetic acuity with line and *nōtan*.

Dow taught three compositional elements: line, color, and *nōtan*. We all know what line and color are, but what about *nōtan*? The term *nōtan* (濃, often translated simply as 'dark-and-light' — or maybe even *chiaroscuro*) was derived from two characters originally used in Chinese and Japanese brush painting: *nō* 濃, which means 'dark, concentrated, undiluted', and *tan* 淡, 'pale' or 'thin'. Together, *nōtan* refers to the varying ink density produced by grinding an ink stick in water. In the hand of a master, a single stroke can produce astonishing variations in tonality, from deep black to silvery gray. In its original context, *nōtan* thus meant more than simple juxtaposition of dark versus light areas. It is the basis for the beautiful nuance in tonality unique to Oriental *sumi-e* painting and brush-and-ink calligraphy.

Georgia O'Keeffe began to experiment with abstract compositions and develop a personal style that veered away from realism. She began to bring to her art what she learned under Dow's tutelage and from Zen Buddhism, specifically simplicity, truth, harmony, and authenticity, a new way of seeing the world.

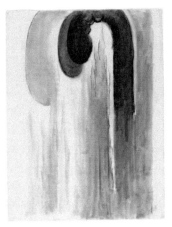

Image 4. *No. 4 Special* (1915)

Image 5. *No. 5 Special* (1915)

Image 6. *No. 8—Special (Drawing No. 8)* (1916)

O'Keeffe started a series of abstract charcoal drawings that were a radical departure from mainstream art and made her one of the first American artists to practice pure abstraction. She called these monochromatic charcoal drawings *Specials*, and she did a series of them from 1914 to 1916. The rich, deep blacks and balance of light and dark, strikingly showed her use of the Zen design principle of *nōtan*.

Image 7. *Winter Road I* (1963)

The oil painting *Winter Road I* is from a much later time (1963) but illustrates O'Keeffe's dedication to simplicity and *nōtan*. Her debt to Arthur Wesley Dow is evident in the subtle gradations of tone and intensity as well as the strong, dominant line in this work and in Dow's *Circle* pictured on page 38.

Throughout her career, O'Keeffe showed a particular affection for certain lines and patterns. They recur often in her paintings. The clearest example is perhaps the 'Y' shape, sometimes inverted like λ, the Greek lambda, that occurs naturally in nature. She used this time and time again in her flowers, animal skulls, landscapes, and other nature paintings.

Image 8. *Red Canna* (1924)

41

Image 9. *Summer Days* (1936)

Image 10. *Black Mesa Landscape,*
New Mexico /Out Back of Marie's II (1930)

Image 11. *Waterfall – No. 1 –*
Iao Valley – Maui (1939)

Image 12. *Winter Cottonwoods East V* (1954)

Another shape that fascinated O'Keeffe was a mesa called Cerro Pedernal that loomed over her New Mexico house. This image recurred in both her representational and more abstract paintings.

Image 13. Georgia O'Keeffe's House in New Mexico

Image 14. *Pedernal with Red Hills* (1936)

Image 15. *Pedernal, 1945*

Note that in Image 15 what looks like a big blue moon is actually the blue sky viewed through an animal pelvis!

Traveling back in time, we come to that point in O'Keeffe's life when she left her schooling and began her career as artist. In 1912, O'Keeffe took a teaching position in the Texas Panhandle, her first exposure to the American Southwest. She lived for two years in Amarillo and later two more years in Canyon, Texas.

Image 16. *Light Coming on the Plains No 1* (1917)

Light Coming on the Plains dates from this period. In addition to the *nōtan* gradations of ink intensity, note the strong use of line and brushwork in the *sumi-e* style. This painting suggests a Zen *ensō* celebrating the liberation of the mind from the body as well as the rising of the sun over West Texas.

Another brush painting, *Blue Lines* from 1916, shows the influence of Japanese calligraphy.

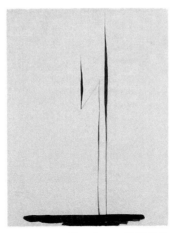

Image 17. *Blue Lines X* (1916)

45

Other 'blue' works from the same year shows O'Keeffe's use of *nōtan* similar to her charcoal drawings.

Image 18. *Blue #1* (1916)

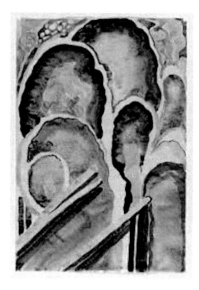

Image 19. *Blue #2* (1916)

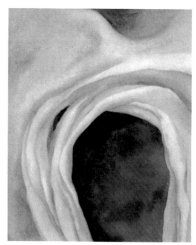

Image 20. *Music—Pink and Blue* (1918)

In these same years, the mid-nineteen-teens, the famed New York photographer and gallery owner Alfred Stieglitz first saw O'Keeffe's drawings, and was immediately moved by their power and energy. Shortly thereafter, from 1916, he exhibited them in '291', his New York City art gallery. The same vitality could be seen in O'Keeffe's early flower images:-

Image 21. *Blue and Green Music* (1921)

Image 22.
Jack-in-the-Pulpit No. IV (1930)

Image 23.
Jimson Weed / White Flower No. 1 (1932)

47

as well as her later work with animal bones against a blue sky:

Image 24. *Pelvis II* (1944)

At Stieglitz's urging, O'Keeffe moved to New York, and they moved in together. They were married in 1924, after Stieglitz divorced his wife. He continued to feature her paintings in his galleries for two decades.

O'Keeffe was entranced by the play of light on Manhattan buildings and produced a series of cityscapes.

Image 25. *The Shelton with Sunspots, N.Y.* (1926)

48

She and Stieglitz summered at Lake George, a resort community north of New York City.

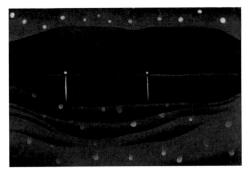

Image 26. *Starlit Night, Lake George 1922*

In 1929, O'Keeffe visited Santa Fe and Taos, New Mexico, both artist colonies. She returned to the state several times to rest and paint, and eventually settled part-year in houses at Ghost Ranch and nearby Abiquiú, north of Santa Fe, in 1940. She moved from New York permanently in 1949. In New Mexico, O'Keeffe was able to realize her ideals – Buddhist ideals really – of simplicity, truth, harmony, and authenticity.

THE SPIRIT OF ZEN

Image 27. Georgia O'Keeffe in her home at Ghost Ranch.
Photograph by John Loengard, 1966.

The spirit of Zen Buddhism in O'Keeffe can be seen in her black and white charcoal drawings; in her use of simple shapes and calligraphic lines; in her use of color and organic forms; in her search for harmony and balance in her work and in her life; and in her constant evocation of the essence and the mystery of her primary subject, which was nature.

49

O'Keeffe followed a singular vision that was authentic to her spirit and very much expressed the tenets of Zen.

The following definition of Zen and art well defines O'Keeffe's goals in her life work:-

> The Zen artist ... tries to suggest by the simplest possible means the inherent nature of the aesthetic object. Anything may be painted, or expressed in poetry, and any sounds may become music. The job of the artist is to suggest the essence, the eternal qualities of the object, which is in itself a work of natural art before the artist arrives on the scene. In order to achieve this, the artist must fully understand the inner nature of the aesthetic object, its Buddha nature. This is the hard part. Technique, though important, is useless without it; and the actual execution of the art work may be startlingly spontaneous, once the artist has comprehended the essence of his subject."[1]

As haiku poets, you all know that the aesthetics of classical Japanese haiku – as well as other Eastern art forms – are quite different from Western aesthetics. That is something that distinguishes haiku from Western poetry. One (or two) key aspects of Japanese aesthetics is/are *wabi* and *sabi*: '*Wabi* is a recognition of the profundity of the humble and everyday; the spirit of poverty'. *Sabi* is 'the spirit of loneliness, the yearning for connection'.

You're feeling *wabi* when for your tea you prefer a chipped old stoneware mug over a shiny, stainless steel cup. *Sabi* might be thought of as a kind of sad but sweet nostalgia. The Russians have a word for a feeling like this – *toska* – that one might use, for example, to describe the music of Rachmaninov. Maybe the Portuguese word *saudade* too. But 'Wabi sabi is not a style defined by superficial appearance. It is an aesthetic ideal, a quiet and sensitive state of mind, attainable by learn-

---

[1] Fredric Lieberman, *Zen Buddhism and Its Relationship to Elements of Eastern and Western Arts.*

50

ing to see the invisible, paring away what is unnecessary, and knowing where to stop'.[2]

Both the art of O'Keeffe and her everyday life were full of *wabi-sabi* (the two related terms are usually fused and hyphenated these days).

The photo in Image 28 shows the central courtyard of O'Keeffe's house in Abiquiú, New Mexico, and the 'black door', another of the shapes that fascinated her. On the right is her 1948 painting of the same view.

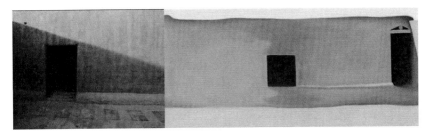

Image 28.
(Left) Photograph of the "black door" at O'Keeffe's house in Abiquiú, N.M.
(Right) *In the Patio IV (Black Door)* by Georgia O'Keeffe (1948)

I wonder if O'Keeffe was aware of, and influenced by, Cubist and Futurist painters such as the Russian Kazimir Malevich, who loved to play with basic geometric shapes in paintings such as *Black Square.*

Image 29. Kazimir Malevich, *Black Square* (1915)

[2] Tim Wong & Akiko Hirano. '侘寂 Wabi Sabi – Learning to See the Invisible'. Touching Stone – Japanese Aesthetics in the Southwest website; http://www.touchingstone.com/Wabi_Sabi.html.

The interiors of O'Keeffe's houses were very simple yet nobly beautiful in their simplicity.

Image 30.
Corner in Georgia O'Keeffe's home.

Among other things, O'Keeffe valued common stones for their texture, shape, and color, and she had several collections at Abiquiú. One is reminded of the Japanese art of *suiseki*, or stone appreciation.

Image 31.
O'Keeffe's stone and shell collections at the Abiquiú house.

She seemed to appreciate all Oriental arts, in fact. She admired the *ukiyo-e* art of Hiroshige and Hokusai, and she studied Chinese ink paintings.

Christine Patten, author of *Miss O'Keeffe*, a biography, wrote: 'Georgia O'Keeffe loved *The Book of Tea*. The similarities between her own life and the Japanese tea ceremony were obvious – her constant manner, her humility, her exactness, her utterly respectful exactness.'

As for haiku, I don't think O'Keeffe ever wrote any verses in Asian style, but she certainly knew of haiku and is thought to have owned books of haiku.

Georgia O'Keeffe made a long trip to Asia in 1959, visiting India, Southeast Asia, and Japan. She returned to Japan the following year and made a number of paintings of Mount Fuji, including this one:

Image 32. *Untitled (Mt. Fuji)* (1960)

I don't think I have ever before seen this iconic Japanese scene rendered in pastel pink! She came back from Japan with kimono, and lots of them. She loved to wear them, open and loose.

Image 33. Bruce Weber, *O'Keeffe* (1984)

O'Keeffe was subject to bouts of illness throughout her life, and she became increasingly frail in her later years. In 1984 she moved into the city of Santa Fe, where she died two years later, at the age of 98.

HAIKU WRITTEN TO O'KEEFFE PAINTINGS

Image 34. *Lake George 1922*

It should not be surprising that Georgia O'Keeffe, preeminent American female artist and New Mexico's favorite daughter, would be the subject of admiration by other artists and poets, haiku poets definitely not excluded. In his section I present all the haiku (and an occasional tanka) that were written about O'Keeffe and her paintings that I could find. These are matched with images of those paintings, as near as I could.

Image 35

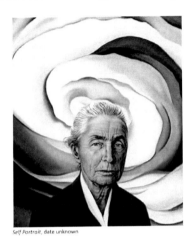

Self Portrait, date unknown

Dead center
in the center of her flowers
Georgia O'Keeffe

Ann Atwood
– *Frogpond* (1989)

Image 36

Sky Above Clouds II, 1963

below the plane
paving the blue expanse
Georgia O'Keeffe clouds

LADavidson – Penumbra Contest 1994

Image 37

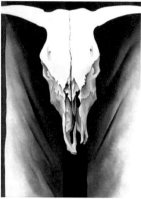

Cow's Skull: Red, White, and Blue, 1931

Under desert stars
a bleached cow skull
fills my dreams

Lynn Edge – Visiting Georgia O'Keeffe
via the Internet, *Frogpond* 37.3

Image 38

Black Iris, 1926

Bodhidarma
taken down and replaced
with O'Keeffe's iris

George Jaramill-Leone – *Frogpond* 9.4

Image 39

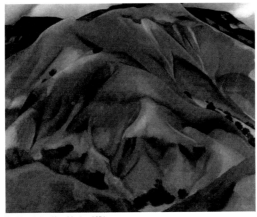

The Mountains, New Mexico, 1951

Georgia O'Keeffe
a splash of brilliant sunset
across the cliffs

Elizabeth Searle Lamb –
Across the Windharp (1999)

Image 40

Herbert Lotz, *The Roofless Room with O'Keeffe Sculpture,* 2007

In Abiquiu
her presence still
Georgia O'Keeffe

Elizabeth Searle Lamb – *Across the Windharp* (1999)

Image 41

Black Door with Red 1954

Almost twilight
brooms at rest
in the adobe courtyard

Anne McKay – *Shaping the Need* (1991)

Image 42

Rose, 1957

and the Dijon roses
wild by the well
...bearing yellow
through two seasons

Anne McKay – *Shaping the Need* (1991)

58

Image 43

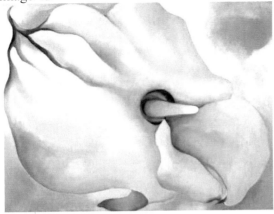

Yellow Calla, 1926

blooming still   o'keeffe's yellos calla

Anne McKay 'shades of yellow (sequence)
Modern Haiku 20:1

Image 44

Yellow calla...
       a new planet
       a nova
           noon sun

Anne McKay
– *Shaping the Need* (1991)

Yellow Calla, 1929

Image 45

children bobbing
through the pelvis
of Georgia O'Keeffe

Raymond Roseliep
– *Rabbit in the Moon* 1983

Title and date unknown

oh, Ray
have you seen her
'Georgia Rose'?

Charles Trumbull (unpublished)

I wrote my haiku upon reading the one by the great American haikuist Father Raymond Roseliep. I can't say that I understand Father Ray's haiku, but I do know that he was much enamored of roses, the redder the better, and used the rose it as a personal symbol (his name, in fact, comes from the German *rose* – 'red' and *lieb* – 'love').

Image 46

over red hills
the colored rings of sunrise
the balance
of moving forward
and letting go

Cyndi Lloyd, *Tinywords* 18.2

Red Hills, Lake George, 1927

Image 47

The street light at 47th
that halo
   still yellow
      to sing me home

   Anne McKay
   Shaping the Need (1991)

New York Street with Moon, 1925

Image 48

            to arrive at the white place…
   only the white wind
            speaks here

   Anne McKay – *Shaping the Need* (1991)

61

Image49 *Oriental Poppies,* 1927

making love:
Georgia O'Keeffe's petals
keep flashing

Charles D.Nethaway, Jr – *Frogpond* 12.1

Image 50

children bobbing
through the pelvis
of Georgia O'Keeffe

Raymond Roesliep
Rabbit in the Moon (1983)

Tony Vaccaro, Georgia O'Keeffe adjusts a canvas (*Red With Yellow,* 1945)
from her Pelvis Series, 1960

Image 51

Blue Morning Glories, 1935

Wishing I
were Georgia O'Keeffe
morning glory

Ann K.Schwader – *Roadrunner* V:1

Image 52

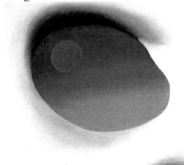

Pelvis IV, 1944

pale moon
through the pelvis of a mule
desert quietude

Charles Trumbull – *A Five-Balloon Morning* (2013)

Image 53

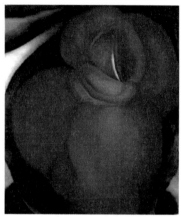

Georgia O'Keeffe Engagement Calendar, 2017

buying a diary –
it's a red-colored picture
by Georgia O'Keeffe

Ikuyo Yoshimura – *Spring Thunder* (1995)

Image 54

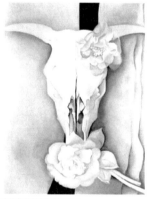

Cow's Skull with Calico Roses, 1931

O'Keeffe's New Mexico;
two steer skulls bleaching
in the desert sun Gloria

H.Procsal – *The Red Pagoda* 2.1

64

O'KEEFFE AS THE SUBJECT OF ARTISTS

Image 55.
Alfred Stieglitz, *Georgia O'Keeffe* (1918)

Photographer Alfred Stieglitz, of course, was O'Keeffe's lover and later her husband. It was he who 'discovered' O'Keeffe and presented her to the East Coast artistic society. In 1918–1921 he undertook a famous series of photographs of her.

Above, the classic studio portrait that we used for at the beginning of this presentation. I love this picture, especially its sensuous overtones.

Second is an informal portrait, but one that is again clearly posed. I find this totally haunting. I can't tell by the look on her face and her robe if she is ill or maybe just getting up …

Image 56.
Alfred Stieglitz, *Georgia O'Keeffe* (1918)

Third, a more playful portrait against the background of one of her paintings:

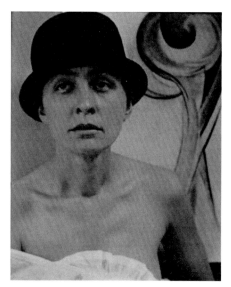

Image 57.
Alfred Stieglitz, *Georgia O'Keeffe* (1918)

Stieglitz lavished attention over every inch of O'Keeffe, from her hands...

Image 58.
Alfred Stieglitz, *Georgia O'Keeffe* (1918)

to her feet ...

Image 59.
Alfred Stieglitz, *Georgia O'Keeffe—Feet* (1918)

and everything in between...

Image 60.
Alfred Stieglitz, *Georgia O'Keeffe—Torso* (1918)

Todd Webb was a protégé of Stieglitz's. He met O'Keeffe in 1946 at an exhibit in Stieglitz's gallery in New York and visited her in New Mexico several times thereafter. Webb's photos of O'Keeffe from the 1960s are mostly apparent informals that show the artist in the places she loved to visit and work. Image 61, for example, shows O'Keeffe at some elevation looking down on the valley of the Chama River – most likely near Ghost Ranch.

Image 61.
Todd Webb, O'Keeffe looking down on
the Chama River Valley, probably at Ghost Ranch (1960s?)

One of O'Keeffe's favorite places to paint was a site about 150 miles north of her house that she called 'Black Place'. The Metropolitan Museum of Art website says "she said [it] looked from a distance, like 'a mile of elephants.'" On page 69 appear her abstract painting, *Black Place II* from 1944, and a Todd Webb photo of her there in the 1960s.

Image 62. *Black Place II* (1944)

Image 63.
Todd Webb, *Georgia O'Keeffe at Black Place* (1963)

Webb also photographed O'Keeffe at her Ghost Ranch house. The following shot, probably posed, was taken there on the *portal* (veranda).

Notice the iconic steer skull, animal bones (or high-desert driftwood?), and rock collection. As always the frame is filled with blacks and whites.

Image 64.
Georgia O'Keeffe on Ghost Ranch Portal, New Mexico (c. 1960s)

And last is perhaps the most famous of all photos of Georgia O'Keeffe – that by Yusuf Karsh:

Image 65.
Yusuf Karsh, Portrait of Georgia O'Keeffe (1956)

Karsh wrote of the experience of photographing an American icon: "I decided to photograph her as another friend had described her: 'Georgia, her pure profile calm, clear; her sleek black hair drawn swiftly back into a tight knot at the nape of her neck; the strong white hands, touching and lifting everything, even the boiled eggs, as if they were living things – sensitive slow-moving hands, coming out of the black and white, always this black and white.'"

Image source citations

1. Georgia O'Keeffe. Photographer: Alfred Stieglitz. Source: School of the Art Institute of Chicago; http://www.saic.edu/150/mother-american-modernism.

2. Arthur Wesley Dow. Photographer and date not given. Historic Ipswich [Mass.] website; https://historicipswich.org/2019/02/01/arthur-wesley-dow/.

3. *Circle* by Arthur Wesley Dow. Ipswich Museum: https://store.ipswichmuseum.org/dir/product/arthur-wesley-dow-circle-2/.

4. *No. 4 Special* by Georgia O'Keeffe. 1915 Charcoal on Fabriano laid paper. Alfred Stieglitz Collection. National Gallery of Art. https://www.nga.gov/collection/art-object-page.75107.html.

5. *No. 5 Special* by Georgia O'Keeffe. 1915 Charcoal on Fabriano laid paper. National Gallery of Art. https://en.wikipedia.org/wiki/Charcoal_drawings_by_Georgia_O%27Keeffe_from_1915#/media/File:Georgia_O'Keefe_No._5_Special_1915_NGA.tif.

6. *No. 8—Special (Drawing No. 8)* by Georgia O'Keeffe,. 1915 Charcoal on paper mounted on cardboard. Whitney Museum of American Art. https://whitney.org/Events/FallCourse2009AmericanAbstractArt.

7. *Winter Road I* by Georgia O'Keeffe. 1963 Oil on canvas. National Gallery of Art. https://www.nga.gov/collection/art-object-page.91449.html.

8. *Red Canna* by Georgia O'Keeffe. 1924 Philadelphia Academy of the Fine Arts. https://wikivisually.com/wiki/Red_Canna_(paintings)

9. *Summer Days* by Georgia O'Keeffe. 1936 Whitney Museum of American Art. https://whitney.org/collection/works/7539.

10. *Black Mesa Landscape, New Mexico / Out Back of Marie's II* by Georgia O'Keeffe. 1930 Oil on canvas mounted on board. The Tate Gallery. https://www.artsy.net/artwork/georgia-okeeffe-black-mesa-landscape-new-mexico-slash-out-back-of-maries-ii.

11. *Waterfall—No. 1—Iao Valley—Maui* by Georgia O'Keeffe. 1939 Oil on canvas. Memphis Brooks Museum of Art. http://www.brooksmuseum.org/georgia-okeeffe-visions-of-hawaii.

71

12. *Winter Cottonwoods East V* by Georgia O'Keeffe. 1954 Georgia O'Keeffe Museum. https://prints.okeeffemuseum.org/detail/460670/okeeffe-winter-cottonwoods-east-v-1954.

13. Georgia O'Keeffe's House in New Mexico. Photographer not stated. *Architectural Digest* website. https://www.architecturaldigest.com/story/okeefe-article-032002

14. *Pedernal with Red Hills*. 1936) by Georgia O'Keeffe. Georgia O'Keeffe Museum. http://www.bbc.com/culture/story/20160705-georgia-okeeffe-pictures.

15. *Pedernal, 1945* by Georgia O'Keeffe. Georgia O'Keeffe Museum. http://adobeairstream.com/art/georgia-okeeffe-and-the-faraway-touch-relics-on-display/.

16. *Light Coming on the Plains No. 1* by Georgia O'Keeffe. 1917 Watercolor on newsprint paper. Amon Carter Museum of American Art, Fort Worth, Texas; https://www.cartermuseum.org/artworks/27408.

17. *Blue Lines X* by Georgia O'Keeffe. 1916), Watercolor and graphite on paper. Alfred Stieglitz Collection, 1969, Metropolitan Museum of Art; https://www.metmuseum.org/art/collection/search/489815.

18. *Blue #1* by Georgia O'Keeffe. 1916 Watercolor and graphite on paper. Brooklyn Museum. https://www.wikiwand.com/en/Georgia_O%27Keeffe.

19. *Blue #2* by Georgia O'Keeffe. 1916) Watercolor and graphite on paper. Brooklyn Museum. https://wikivisually.com/wiki/Charcoal_drawings_by_Georgia_O%27Keeffe_from_1915.

20. *Music—Pink and Blue* by Georgia O'Keeffe. 1918 Oil on canvas. Museum of Modern Art. https://www.moma.org/interactives/exhibitions/2012/inventingabstraction/?work=174.

21. *Blue and Green Music* by Georgia O'Keeffe. 1921 Oil on canvas. The Art Institute of Chicago. https://en.wikipedia.org/wiki/Blue_and_Green_Music#/media/File:Blue-green.jpg

22. *Jack-in-the-Pulpit No. IV* by Georgia O'Keeffe. 1930 Oil on canvas. Alfred Stieglitz Collection, National Gallery of Art. https://www.nga.gov/collection/art-object-page.70179.html

23. *Jimson Weed / White Flower No. 1* by Georgia O'Keeffe. 1932)

24. *Pelvis II* by Georgia O'Keeffe. 1944 Oil on canvas. Pinterest website; https://www.pinterest.com/pin/94786767128398605/?lp=true

25. *The Shelton with Sunspots, N.Y.* by Georgia O'Keeffe. 1926 The Art institute of Chicago. https://www.artic.edu/artworks/104031/the-shelton-with-sunspots-n-y.

26. *Starlit Night, Lake George 1922* by Georgia O'Keeffe. Oil on canvas. Private Collection (image © Georgia O'Keeffe Museum/Artists Rights Society (ARS), New York). https://namhenderson.wordpress.com/2013/09/01/starlight-night-lake-george-1922/.

27. Georgia O'Keeffe in her home at Ghost Ranch. Photograph by John Loengard, 1968. https://www.pinterest.com/pin/13933080067215036/?lp=true.

28. (Left) Photograph of the "black door" at O'Keeffe's house in Abiquiú, N.M. Photographer and date unknown. (Right) *In the Patio IV (Black Door)* by Georgia O'Keeffe, 1948. https://curiator.com/art/georgia-okeeffe/in-the-patio-iv-black-door

29. *Black Square*, Kazimir Malevich, 1915. Photographer unknown. From the Tate Modern show in 2014. https://www.widewalls.ch/kazimir-malevich-black-square-racist-note/.

30. Corner in Georgia O'Keeffe's home. Photographer and date unknown. https://www.google.com/search?q=Georgia+O%27keeffe%27s+home+images&tbm=isch&source=hp&sa=X&ved=2ahUKEwix9eXukpzkAhXFjp4KHQXmBbQQ7Al6BAgEECQ&biw=1070&bih=943#imgrc=QWJaQBLA_rn2WM. Image no longer available.

31. O'Keeffe's stone and shell collections at the Abiquiú house. Photographer and date unknown. https://leslieparke.com/georgia-mind-visit-georgia-okeeffes-home-landscape/.

32. Untitled (Mt. Fuji) by Georgia O'Keeffe, 1960. Georhia O'Keeffe Museum: https://www.okeeffemuseum.org/wp-content/uploads/2016/07/CR1447-1140x667.jpg.

33. *O'Keeffe*. Photographer: Bruce Weber, Abiquiú, N.M., 1984. © Bruce Weber and Nan Bush Collection. https://www.ft.com/content/bc2dd90a-12dc-11e7-b0c1-37e417ee6c76.

34. *Lake George, 1922* by Georgia O'Keeffe. Oil on canvas. San Francisco Museum of Modern Art, Gift of Charlotte Mack (image © Georgia O'Keeffe Museum/Artist Rights Society (ARS), New York). https://hyperallergic.com/75531/a-painters-retreat-georgia-okeeffe-and-lake-george/

35. *Self Portrait*, date unknown. https://www.pinterest.com/pin/246712885822831174/. *Note:* There is so little information and so few copies of this image on the Web that is seems possible this is not an original O'Keeffe work.

36. *Sky Above Clouds II* by Georgia O'Keeffe, 1963. Private Collection. https://www.etsy.com/listing/594270876/georgia-okeeffe-sky-above-clouds-ii-art.

37. *Cow's Skull: Red, White, and Blue*, 1931. Oil on canvas. Alfred Stieglitz

73

Collection, 1952, The Metropolitan Museum of Art.
https://www.metmuseum.org/toah/works-of-art/52.203/

38. *Black Iris* by Georgia O'Keeffe, 1926. Oil on canvas. Alfred Stieglitz Collection, Metropolitan Museum of Art.
https://en.wikipedia.org/wiki/Black_Iris_(painting).

39. *The Mountain, New Mexico* by Georgia O'Keeffe. 1931.
https://www.flickr.com/photos/jonathanbarker/3181494251/. Note: this painting is called *The Mountains, New Mexico* and dated 1951 on the commercial website
http://artgaga.com/index.php?route=product/product&product_id=25795.

40. *Georgia O'Keeffe's house in Abiquiú, New Mexico.* Photograph by Herb Lotz, 2007. ©Georgia O'Keeffe Museum. https://www
.knoll.com/knollnewsdetail/georgia-okeeffe-abiquiu-new-mexico

41. *Black Door with Red* by Georgia O'Keeffe, 1954. Bequest of Walter P. Chrysler, Jr., Ontario Museum of Art.
https://www.theglobeandmail.com/arts/art-and-architecture/ago-exhibit-reframes-georgia-okeeffe-as-a-pioneeringabstractionist/article34776145/

42. *Rose* by Georgia O'Keeffe. 1957. No other information available.
https://www.pinterest.com/pin/63543044723268193/?lp=true

43. *Yellow Calla* by Georgia O'Keeffe. 1926. Oil on fiberboard. Smithsonian American Art Museum, Gift of the Woodward Foundation.
https://americanart.si.edu/artwork/yellow-calla-18900

44. *Yellow Calla* by Georgia O'Keeffe. 1929. No other information available.
https://66.media.tumblr.com/215bc09e490550c7375fdbaec74d11cf/tumblr_o39 n9iLVeI1s4zvvyo1_640.jpg

45. No information available.
https://cinematicpassions.files.wordpress.com/2010/09/3551633876_851cb78e7 d_z.jpg

46. *Red Hills, Lake George* by Georgia O'Keeffe. 1927. Oil on canvas. The Phillips Collection. © The Georgia O'Keeffe Foundation / Artists Rights Society (ARS), New York.
https://www.phillipscollection.org/research/american_art/artwork/OKeeffe-Red_Hills.htm

47. *New York Street with Moon* by Georgia O'Keeffe, 1925. Oil on canvas. Carmen Thyssen-Bornemisza Collection on loan at the Museo Nacional Thyssen-Bornemisza, Madrid.
https://www.museothyssen.org/en/collection/artists/okeeffe-georgia/new-york-street-moon

48. *From the White Place* by Georgia O'Keeffe, 1940. Oil on canvas. The Phillips Collection © The Georgia O'Keeffe Foundation / Artists Rights Society

74

(ARS), New York.
https://www.phillipscollection.org/research/american_art/artwork/OKeeffe-From_White_Place.htm

49. *Oriental Poppies* by Georgia O'Keeffe. 1927. Oil on canvas. Weisman Art Museum. https://en.wikipedia.org/wiki/Oriental_Poppies_(painting)

50. Georgia O'Keeffe adjusts a canvas (*Red With Yellow*, 1945) from her Pelvis Series. Photographer: Tony Vaccaro, 1960. Monroe Galley of Photography: https://monroegallery.blogspot.com/2017/03/tony-vaccaro-on-panel-at-brooklyn.html.

51. *Blue Morning Glories* by Georgia O'Keeffe. 1935. Location not found. http://thehiddengemm.blogspot.com/2015/01/art-eye-blue-morning-glories-georgia.html

52. *Pelvis IV* by Georgia O'Keeffe. 1944. The Georgia O'Keeffe Museum: https://www.okeeffemuseum.org/installation/okeeffes-new-mexico/.

53. Cover of the *2017 Georgia O'Keeffe Engagement Calendar* (Poster Revolution, 2016). The image is *Red Flower*, 1919. Oil on Canvas. Norton Museum of Art. See https://www.artsy.net/artwork/georgia-okeeffe-red-flower.

54. *Cow's Skull with Calico Roses* by Georgia O'Keeffe. 1931. The Art Institute of Chicago: https://www.artic.edu/artworks/61428/cow-s-skull-with-calico-roses

55. *Georgia O'Keeffe*. Photographer: Alfred Stieglitz. School of the Art Institute of Chicago: http://www.saic.edu/150/mother-american-modernism.

56. *Portrait of Georgia O'Keeffe*. Photographer: Alfred Stieglitz. 1918. Palladium print. Alfred Stieglitz Collection, The Art Institute of Chicago: https://media.artic.edu/stieglitz/portfolio_page/georgia-okeeffe-1918-2/.

57. *Georgia O'Keeffe*. Photographer: Alfred Stieglitz. 1918. Palladium print. Alfred Stieglitz Collection, The Art Institute of Chicago: https://media.artic.edu/stieglitz/portfolio_page/georgia-okeeffe-1918-3/.

58. *Georgia O'Keeffe*. Photographer: Alfred Stieglitz. 1918. Gelatin silver print. Alfred Stieglitz Collection, The Art Institute of Chicago: https://media.artic.edu/stieglitz/portfolio_page/georgia-okeeffe-1918/.

59. *Georgia O'Keeffe—Feet*. Photographer: Alfred Stieglitz. 1918. Gelatin silver print. Alfred Stieglitz Collection, The Art Institute of Chicago: https://media.artic.edu/stieglitz/portfolio_page/georgia-okeeffe-feet-1918/.

60. *Georgia O'Keeffe—Torso, 1918*. Photographer: Alfred Stieglitz. 1918. Gelatin silver print. Alfred Stieglitz Collection, The Art Institute of Chicago: https://media.artic.edu/stieglitz/portfolio_page/georgia-okeeffe-torso-1918/.

61. O'Keeffe looking down on the Chama River Valley, probably at Ghost Ranch, 1960s? Photographer: Todd Webb. Georgia O'Keeffe Museum: https://www.okeeffemuseum.org/installation/todd-webb/.

62. *Black Place II*, 1944 by Georgia O'Keeffe. Alfred Stieglitz Collection, Metropolitan Museum of Art. https://www.metmuseum.org/art/collection/search/489063.

63. *Georgia at Black Place*. Photographer: Todd Webb, 1963. Georgia O'Keeffe Museum: https://www.okeeffemuseum.org/store/products/posters/photography-posters/georgia-at-black-place-1963/.

64. Todd Webb, *Georgia O'Keeffe on Ghost Ranch Portal, New Mexico*, circa 1960s. © Estate of Todd Webb. https://kinfolk.com/georgia-okeeffe-living-modern/.

65. *Georgia O'Keeffe*. Photographer: Yusuf Karsh, 1956. Georgia O'Keeffe house, Abiquiú, N.M. https://karsh.org/photographs/georgia-okeeffe/.

RH BLYTH (1898-1964) AND HIS INFLUENCE IN THE MODERN HAIKU WORLD
The Relationship between RH Blyth and James W Hackett (1929-2015)

Ikuyo Yoshimura(PhD)

Before I make my speech on RH Blyth, I'd like to thank Colin Blundell, Iliyana Stoyanova, David Bingham and members of *The British Haiku Society* for inviting me to this conference.

About 25 years ago, I stayed in Cambridge as the escorting teacher for college students. At that time, David Cobb, who started up the BHS, visited me to ask me to become a member of the Society. With my pleasure, I became a member at that time. When David came to see me I had been a contributor to Kevin Bailey's *Haiku Quarterly*, the first Haiku magazine in England. David Cobb gave me great help for my research on RH Blyth. Though I'd been studying RH Blyth for over 20 years, I could not have completed my research without the great help of David Cobb, James Kirkup, James W Hackett and Blyth's relatives. Especially Blyth's daughters, Harumi and Nana, who gave deep understanding to my research.

And I now meet many friends here: Charles Trumbull, a companionship of many years, David Lanoue, Zen haiku scholar, my close Polish friend, Marta M Chocilowska and Ms Kitabukuro from Japan gathered together here at this conference. I believe I can make precious friends in the world through haiku. And haiku friends bring me into a rich and brilliant world. My speech will consist of the following sections:-

1 Encountering RH Blyth
2 Blyth's works in Japan
3 Blyth's influence on American Haiku
4 James W Hackett as pupil of Blyth
5 Blyth's prediction about world haiku
6 Photos of Blyth, his family and James W Hackett

1 Encountering RH Blyth

Two factors influenced me to begin to study the British-born scholar RH Blyth.

First, was an interest in his haiku translations and his view of haiku that I needed for composing my own haiku in English as well as translating Japanese haiku into English.

Second, in June 1993, James Kirkup, who was then president of *The British Haiku Society* (BHS) and David Cobb, secretary general, asked me to research Blyth's life in Japan. He had lived in Japan for 40 years after leaving England at the age of 24 (16 years in Korea, and 24 years on the Japanese mainland). The BHS had only limited information about him at that time. Even the reference library of the University of London, from which Blyth graduated, had only the list of his works and some obituary articles.

I am very glad that the BHS garnered so much information and new facts in order to publish *The Genius of Haiku: Readings from RH Blyth*. This book is, so to speak, a Renaissance of the works of RH Blyth. In addition, I was very happy to help the BHS in researching information on him. Kirkup was writing an introduction about Blyth for *The Genius of Haiku*. My intensive studies of RH Blyth began at that time.

The Genius of Haiku was published in April 1994 to commemorate the 300th anniversary of Bashō's death and the 30th anniversary of Blyth's death. It is a book of 146 pages comprising Kirkup's introduction as the foreword and extracts from Blyth's books:-

> *Haiku*
> *Zen in English Literature and Oriental Classics*
> *A History of Haiku*
> *Zen and Zen Classics*
> *Japanese Life and Character in Senryū*

The Genius of Haiku is a guidebook to the study of Blyth for worldwide haiku poets. I think its publication was like a first home-

78

coming for Blyth to his motherland after leaving in 1924. My speech is perhaps his second homecoming to England!

In 1996, two years after the publication of *The Genius of Haiku*, I wrote my own publication on Blyth, *The Life of RH Blyth who loved Zen and Haiku* (Dohosha1996).

One day James W Hackett advised me that I should send it to Emperor Akihito, who retired from the Imperial Throne on April 30th 2019, Blyth's longest student. Blyth had the Emperor as his student for a few years before the Emperor got married. Fortunately I had the opportunity to meet Empress Michiko at the Poetry Reading Circle in Tokyo and handed her *The Life of RH Blyth* which was written as my research. I was grateful that Hackett suggested this to me.

2 Blyth's work in Japan

Japanese haiku verse has been translated by diplomats or foreign hired teachers, such as Basil Hall Chamberlain, Lafcadio Hearn, and Paul Louis Couchoud, who were interested in Japanese culture and Japanese literature in the Meiji Era (1868-1912), and haiku has now become well-known in Western countries. There were also a few examples of haiku translations into English by Japanese scholars, such as Asataro Miyamori and Yonejiro Noguchi, but haiku was not so positively regarded by the Japanese as it was by foreigners.

Haiku in English got its real start in the fifties, when an avid interest in Japanese culture and religion swept postwar United States. Growing out of the increased contact with Japan through the Occupation and a spiritual thirst for religious and artistic fulfilment, this interest centered on art, literature, and Zen Buddhism. Alan Watts, Donald Keene, DT Suzuki, the Beat Generation, and others contributed to both arousing and feeding this interest, but Cor van den Heuvel described the spread of haiku in the States as being the result of RH Blyth's extraordinary four-volume work *Haiku* (1949-1952), Kenneth Yasuda's *The Japanese Haiku* (1957), and Harold G Henderson's *An Introduction to Haiku* (1958) which provided for the first time the solid foundation necessary for creation of haiku in English.

79

Overseas transmission of haiku after World War II was the result of the work of RH Blyth. With his poetic thought and Zen Buddhism, he translated an immense number of classical Japanese haiku and senryu into English and introduced them overseas. He had great language skill in Latin, Spanish, French, Chinese, Korean and Japanese.

In addition, Blyth is known for drafting, along with Harold Henderson, the Emperor Showa's announcement of his own human status in 1946, helped to ensure the continuation of Gakushuin as a private university, and played an important part as a secret messenger between the Imperial Household Agency and GHQ. In his days in Korea, Blyth studied Zen through the books of Daisetz T Suzuki. After coming to Japan, he studied and practised Zen under Suzuki who spread Zen overseas. As an introduction to the genre, almost all poets who write haiku around the world read the four volumes of Blyth's *Haiku*.

After WWII, Suzuki and Blyth spread haiku throughout Europe and North America, and pointed to the connection of haiku with Zen Buddhism. The Beats, Jack Kerouac, Allen Snyder, Richard Snyder, Richard Wright and James Hackett made big waves in the poetry world of the United States in the 1950's and 1960's, and were particularly strongly influenced by Blyth's works.

This was specially the case with James Hackett, a Zen haiku master in the States who had for his motto, 'the way of haiku is the way of man' and wrote with the understanding that haiku equals Zen.

None among these early writers failed to read Blyth's *Haiku* in four volumes, and they learned from his books that 'haiku is Zen Buddhism'. With the Zen Buddhism boom in the United States, Blyth's books assumed something of the aura of holy books for haiku poets during the days in 1950's and 60's when haiku was accepted in the States. Therefore, it can justly be said that haiku are composed extensively throughout the world today under Blyth's influence. Blyth once said haiku is Japan's greatest gift to the world. But at the present time the Internet is the most useful tool to study and learn haiku.

3 Blyth's Influence on American Haiku

What influence has Blyth's view of haiku – haiku as Zen Buddhism – had on poets in the United States? Blyth notes that:-

Haiku record what Wordsworth calls these 'spots of time', those moments which for some quite mysterious reason have a peculiar significance. There is a unique quality about the poet's state of feeling on these occasions; it may be very deep, it may be rather shallow, but there is a 'something' about the external things, a 'something' about the inner mind which is unmistakable. Where haiku poets excel all others is in recognizing this 'something' in the most unlikely places and at the most unexpected times. (RH Blyth, *Haiku*, Vol.1 The Hokuseido Press 1949 p.8)

Blyth's idea, 'moments which have a peculiar significance', influenced American haiku poets in forming the concepts of 'the essence of a moment', 'the here and now', and 'the haiku moment'. Suzuki introduces Blyth's view of haiku in his *Zen and Japanese Culture*: '...To quote Dr RH Blyth, an authority on the study of haiku: 'A haiku is the expression of temporary enlightenment, in which we see into the life of things.' Whether 'temporary' or not, Bashō gives his seventeen syllables a significant intuition into Reality...' Blyth recognized that haiku and Zen Buddhism were two sides of the same coin.

This 'flash of enlightenment' caught the hearts of American poets, and the haiku moment became one of the characteristics of American haiku.

Blyth says in other words that this 'something' is 'awareness' based on a sharp recognition power. Awareness means that what cannot be seen can be seen. It means finding something that is overlooked and unnoticed. It means an unexpected discovery

In their *Draft Definitions Submitted for Member Comment*, The Haiku Society of America offers a definition of haiku as 'A poem recording the essence of a moment keenly perceived, in which nature is linked to human nature'. In addition, in their *Information and Guidelines,* the Haiku Society of America notes that '...haiku must be brief, fresh,

81

using clear images to express the essence of haiku – the 'suchness' of the moment...' This 'suchness' means the fundamental essence and the immanent essence – that is to say, appearance just as it is. In other words, 'suchness' is the appearance of the natural world just as it is, human beings included. Thus, the aim of American haiku is to express clearly the essence of a moment in the natural world.

4 James Hackett as pupil of Blyth

James Hackett respected Blyth as a teacher of haiku and as a teacher of the way of life; he concluded that the essence of haiku is 'suchness'. Hackett had been creating haiku since his days as an undergraduate. He sent his haiku to Blyth in around 1957–58. The close friendship between the two men continued until Blyth's death in 1964. When Hackett experienced a life-threatening accident, he received a strong push toward the creation of haiku. Confronting physical pain and conscious of death, Hackett acknowledged the existence of the 'eternal now' and the singular importance of a life that would never recur. He became able to find the solemn beauty of nature and value in every moment by being more obedient to his senses rather than thinking about life abstractly. He found that the creation of haiku was the best means to express the love of living, focusing attention on nature and the moment. For Hackett, the creation of haiku was the learning of Zen Buddhism itself. Blyth notes that 'haiku is the literature which transcended the literature, in a sense, it is literatureless literature...' Or, '...put another way, haiku is not to create a poem but to live...' Blyth's influence can clearly be seen in Hackett's view of haiku.

In a letter to Hackett, Blyth praised the younger man for the essence of his haiku, especially

A tiny spider
has begun to confiscate
this cup's emptiness.

Blyth wrote, '...These all appealed to me strongly, for different reasons. I found a feeling of regret creeping over me as I read through the verses again, and when I thought what it arose from, I realized that it was that Bashō should not have you for his pupil, (and he as your pupil) instead of the rather mediocre disciples he actually had...' (first letter from Blyth to Hackett in 1958)

Furthermore, in his *History of Haiku* (vol. 2 p.351) Blyth introduces Hackett as a leading poet of world haiku: 'These are in no way mere imitations of Japanese haiku, nor literary diversions. They are [aimed at] the Zen experience, the realizing, the making real in oneself of the thing-in-itself, impossible to rational thought, but possible, 'all poets believe,' in experience...'

As for the technique of haiku creation, however, Hackett's opinion differs from Blyth. Blyth checked Hackett's haiku and advised him to omit adjectives and articles as much as possible and to make the whole haiku simple. Hackett, however, persisted in his views. He stated the details in a letter to me (19 August 1997):-

On a more important level, Blyth and I differ slightly on one major point: how the haiku experience could best be expressed in English by an American poet. Blyth believed that haiku in English should be almost as simply expressed as a haiku written in Japanese, that is, with just the fewest words possible. I have always believed that because of profound cultural and linguistic differences, haiku written in language other than Japanese should be expressed in the other culture's natural usage/syntax. Only in this way will world haiku achieve respect and success. Certainly, I believe that simple language and brevity should be the keystone of haiku writing in any language. However, some articles and modifiers (adjectives, adverbs, etc.) should be used if they help the reader to understand and appreciate the haiku moment the poet wishes to share. It is in the art of expression that haiku writing can become poetry. To properly suggest the 'haiku experience' requires much contemplation, spiritual empathy, communion, and very careful word choice by the poet. However, I believe the soul of haiku (its spirit of Zen) is far more important that its form or style of writing.

Hackett thinks that haiku is a form of poetry that can be expressed by people in any country. As he says in *The Zen Haiku and other Zen Poems*, 'The best haiku are created from direct and immediate experience with nature, and that this intuitive experience can be expressed in any language. In essence I regard haiku as fundamentally existential and experiential, rather than literary...'

5 Blyth's prediction about world haiku

In the last chapter of *A History of Haiku* (1964 p.349), published just before his death, Blyth states the premise of 'world haiku' as follows:-

The latest development in the history of haiku is one which nobody foresaw – the writing of haiku outside Japan, not in the Japanese language. We may now assert with some confidence that the day is coming when haiku will be written in Russia, in the Celebes, in Sardinia. What a pleasing prospect, what an Earthly Paradise it will be, the Esquimaux blowing on their fingers as they write haiku about the sun that never sets or rises, the pygmies composing jungle haiku on the gorilla and the python, the nomads of Sahara and Gobi deserts seeing a grain of sand in the world!

His prediction comes true and haiku poets now born in Mongolia, Africa, and places with non-native speakers of English. Yes, about fifty-five years ago Blyth predicted what world haiku would be like.

6 Photos – RH Blyth and his family

Blyth's parents

Blyth's daughters, Harumi & Nana, at Blyth's grave in Kita Kamakura

85

Blyth's family in Tokyo

Other Photos

David Cobb in 1994 on the launch of *The Genius of Haiku*

86

James Kirkup and the headmaster of Blyth's Junior High School in Ilford 1994

James Hackett and Ikuyo Yoshimura 1996

87

Hackett & Pat with Nana's family in Oiso, Japan 2002

Chronology of RH Blyth composed by Ikuyo Yoshimura

1898 December 3 – born in Leyton, Essex to Horace Blyth & Henrietta Blyth. Birthplace 93 Trumpington Road, Leyton. Nowadays Leyton is called Leytonstone. Blyth and his parents move to Ilford a few miles east from Leyton during his infant days.

1903 (aged 5) – Cleveland Road School: seven grade elementary school.

1910 (aged 13) – County High School: five grade junior high school.

1914 (16) – 1914 to 1916, uncertificated pupil-teacher, teaching French, Spanish and English at Highbury Park School located in the north of London.

1916 (18) – graduated from Junior High School. Imprisoned in Wormwood Scrubs as a conscientious objector [CO] to World War I.

1919 (21) – released from prison. Taught at Cleveland Road School for six months as uncertificated pupil-teacher.

1920 (22) – entered University College, London.

1923 (25) – graduated at top of English literature major of the university. A Japanese student, Mr. Akio Fujii asked Blyth if he wanted to teach English as a foreign teacher at University of Gyungsung after graduating from University College London. Blyth promptly accepted the offer.

1924 (26) – **June** – got a teaching licence at the London Day Training College and got married to Annie Bercovitch, (Jewish English). In **August**, they landed at Kobe in Japan. From **September**, Blyth taught English and English literature at University of Gyungsung.

1926 (28) – lectured in English literature at University of Gyungsung. Blyth and his wife resided at Gyenggi-do, Goyang-Gun, Sungin-Myeon, Jeonnong-Li, Korea.

1927 (29) – impressed by *Essays in Zen Buddhism, First Series* by Daisetz Suzuki (Luzac and Company, London 1927), Blyth became a disciple of Zen through Suzuki's Zen books. In **August**, Blyth had two poems in *The London Mercury*.

1930 (32) – **April**, taught at Gyungsung Commerce High School as a part time teacher. At this time, his father Horace Blyth died. Asataro Miyamori's *One Thousand Haiku Ancient and Modern* (Dobunsha) was published.

1932 (34) – **April**, met Shounosuke Shinki, who came to Gyungsung Commerce High School as a teacher. They became good friends. Asataro Miyamori's *An Anthology of Haiku, Ancient Haiku and Modern* (Maruzen Company) was published.

1933 @ 35 – **April**, adopted son, Lee Insoo entered Gyungsung Commerce High School. HG Henderson's *The Bamboo Broom* was published. At this time Blyth asked Mrs. Motoko Fujii to tutor him in haiku learning.

1934 (36) –**April**, his wife, Annie went back England with adopted son, Lee Insoo.

1935 (37) March, Blyth went back to England and was divorced from Annie. He was impressed by *The Tao Te Ching* by Lao Tzu. English translation, *The Way and its Power* (1934) was made by Arthur Waley.

1936 (38) – **March**, Blyth was back in Gyungsung and taught English at preparatory course of University of Gyungsung, and Gyungsun Commerce High School. He rented a house in Gyungsung-Shi, Ewha-Jung. He stayed there until 1940 when he left for mainland of Japan.

1937 (39) – **March**, Blyth married Miss Tomiko Kurushima.

1938 (40) – Blyth practised religious austerities of Zen Buddhism under Kazan Taigi Roshi at Myosinji temple in Gyungsung. He composed Japanese haiku 'snail'. Daisetz Suzuki's *Zen Buddhism and Its Influence on Japanese Culture* was published.

1939 (41) – **March**, he was removed from Gyungsun Commerce High School. June 28, he filed a first application to be naturalized in Japan to the Goverment. **September 3**, England and France declared war against Germany. World War II broke out.

1940 (42) – **March 21**, Blyth's friend, Akio Fujii, Professor of preparatory course of University of Gyungsung, who had invited Blyth to Gyungsun passed away from angina pectoris at the age of 42. **April**, Blyth and his wife Tomiko moved to Hagi, Yamaguchi prefecture, which was Tomiko's hometown. They stayed there for three months. **August**, they moved to Tokyo. **November**, Blyth was removed from lecturer of preparatory course of University of Gyungsung. He became a foreign teacher of the Fourth Kanazawa High School. They stayed at the official residence of the school and he wrote *Zen in English Literature and Oriental Classics*.

1941 (43) – **April**, Blyth again filed an application for naturalisation to the Japanese Government. But his application only got through the first stage. **May**, the manuscript of *Zen in English Literature and Oriental Classics* was done. The Hokuseido Publishing Company supported its publication. Blyth came face to face with Daisetz Suzuki for the first time in Kanazawa (the date was from November 1940 to December

90

1941). **December 8**, the Pacific War broke out. Blyth was kept in the Naka Police Station in Kanazawa.

1942 (44) – February, Blyth's first daughter, Harumi, was born. March, he was removed from the Forth Kanazawa High School and was institutionalized in The Eastern Lodge Hotel in Kobe as an alien foreign national. December, *Zen in English Literature and Oriental Classics* was published by the Hokuseido Publishing Company. Hokuseido helped to publish almost all his publications even in war time.

1943 (45) – Blyth was moved to the dormitory of Canadian School in Kobe.

1944 (46) – War inmates who were spread around Kobe were gathered together in the building used as a war camp at Futatabi Park in Kobe. There Robert Aitken met Blyth.

1945 (47) – August, Japan defeated and surrendered. Inmates released from the war camp. Blyth and his family stayed with Lewis William Bush in Kobe, who also was in the camp with Blyth.
October, they went up to Tokyo and visited Daisetz Suzuki and Takeshi Saito, professor of Tokyo University. Blyth also visited Harold Henderson who was Lieutenant colonel at Civil Information and Education Section in GHQ (General Headquarters) and a lover of haiku.
November, through recommendation of Takeshi Saito, Blyth had a teaching position at Gakushuin as a foreign teacher. Gakushuin was a kind of educational school for royal and noble families. At that time, Blyth worked for the Imperial House under Katsunoshin Yamanashi, the principal of Gakushuin. Blyth worked on keeping Gakushuin going. Shigeru Yoshida, the Minister of Foreign Affairs, entrusted the task of being a messenger between GHQ and Japanese Government to Blyth. December, Harold Henderson composed the draft of the main part of *Imperial Declaration of Humanity*. Using the draft, Blyth composed an English version.

1946 (48) – January 1, Imperial Rescript, Imperial Declaration of Humanity, wherein Hirohito renounced the imperial claim to divinity. **April**, Blyth became Prince Akihito's tutor. Blyth continued this work until his death in 1964. He also taught English at the training centre of the Ministry of Foreign Affairs, Tokyo University, Nihon University as a concurrent professor. **July**, Daisetz Suzuki & Blyth published *The Cultural East Vol.1, No.1* by Matsugaoka Bunko in Kita Kamakura. **October**, Blyth taught English at Tokyo Educational University. Elizabeth Janet Gray Vining came to Japan as a tutor of Prince Akihito. **November 3**, the Government proclaimed the new constitution.

1947 (49) – **July**, his second daughter, Nana, was born. **August**, *The Cultural East, Vol.1/2* was published.

1948 (50) – taught English at Jissen Women's University, Waseda University, and worked at Jiyu Gakuen College as a part time teacher. **March**, *Dorothy Wordsworth's Journal* was published. **August**, *The New Vista English Readers Senior I* was published. **November**, *RL Stevenson's Will O' the Mill* was published. Blyth proofread Daisetz Suzuki's *Living in Zen*.

1949 (51) – **January**, Blyth & Ichiro Nishizaki published *Workbook of English Examination for National University*. **April**, *Selection from Thoreau's Journals* was published. **August**, *Haiku Volume I: Eastern Culture* was published. **September**, *An Outline of English Literature*, *William Hazlitt: An Anthology*, and *The Poems of Emerson: A Selection* were published. **October**, *A Chronological Anthology of Nature in English Literature* was published. **November**, *Senryu: Japanese Satirical Verses* was published.

1950 (52) – **March**, Blyth & Lee Wang published *The First Book of Korean*. **August**, *Haiku Volume II: Spring* was published. **September**, *An Anthology of Nineteenth Century Prose* was published. **October**, Blyth & Kiji Yoshida published *Senryu: World Satire* in Japanese. **November**, Elizabeth Janet Gray Vining went back to the States. **December**, *Thoughts on Culture – or, How to Be a Human Being* – was published.

1951 (53) – **April**, *A Shortened Version of A Week on the Concord and Merrimack Rivers by Henry David Thoreau* was published. **September**, *A Chronological Anthology of Religion in English Literature* was published. **October**, *English Through Questions & Answers* was published.

1952 (54) – **January**, *HAIKU Volume III: Summer-Autumn*. **April**, *An Anthology of English Poetry*. **May**, *HAIKU Volume IV: Autumn-Winter*. **July**, *Buddhist Sermons on Christian Texts* were published.

1953 (55) – April, *RL Stevenson: Fables* was published. **June**, *A Short History of English Literature* was published. Blyth met Bernard Howell Leach, ceramicist, for the first time in Tokyo.

1954 (56) – **November**, Blyth got a PhD from Tokyo University as a result of *Zen in English Literature and Oriental Classics* and *HAIKU I, II, III, IV*. He planned to go England temporarily, but he couldn't get enough money from Japanese Government and he gave up the plan.

1957 (59) – **October**, *Japanese Humour* was published.

1958 (60) – **April**, *A Survey of English Literature* and *How to Read English Poetry* were published.

1959 (61) – **March**, *Easy Poems, Book One* and *Easy Poems, Book Two* were published. **May**, *Oriental Humour* and *Humour in English Literature: A Chronological Anthology* were published. Blyth was decorated with the Fourth Order Zuihosho for his achievements by the Japanese Government. **August**, he got permission to get a foreign Order from Queen of England. He bought his own house at Oiso, Kanagawa with the help of Katsunoshin Yamanashi. He and his family moved to Oiso from Gakushuin teachers' house in Mejiro.

1960 (62) – **March**, *Zen and Zen Classics, Volume I: General Introduction, From the Upanishads to Huineng* was published. **April**, *More English through Questions & Answers* was published.

1961 (63) – **February**, *Japanese Life and Character in Senryu* was published. **September**, *Edo Satirical Verse Anthologies* was published.

1962 (64) – **May**, *Zen and Zen Classics, Volume V: Twenty-five Zen Essays* was published.

1963 (65) – **October**, *A History of Haiku, Volume I: From the Beginnings up to Issa* was published.

1964 (66) – **June**, Blyth hospitalized in the Kyoundo Hospital in Hiratsuka, Kanagawa. **July**, he left the hospital. *A History of Haiku, Volume II: From Issa up to the Present* and *Zen and Zen Classics, Volume II: History of Zen* were published. **September**, he was hospitalized in the St. Luke Hospital, Tokyo. **October**, he was moved to the Seiwa Hospital, Tokyo. **October 28**, he passed away as a result of a brain tumour. **November 1**, his funeral ceremony was performed at the Library in Gakushuin University. He was buried near Daisetz Suzuki's grave in Tokeiji, Kita Kamakura.

His posthumous Buddhist name is 'Blyth, the person who shone the way of Zen and its spirit...'

Publications after Blyth died
1966 *Zen and Zen Classics, Volume IV*: Mumonkan .
1970 *Zen and Zen Classics, Volume III: History of Zen, Nangaku Branch*

GENDAI ISSA   David G. Lanoue

Gendai: *A Japanese word that signifies 'nowadays', 'modern era,' 'modern times', and 'present-day'.*

In 2017 I published a how-to-write haiku book titled, *Write Like Issa*. It was based on a series of ten workshops that I gave in ten different cities in the United States over a period of five years. In those workshops, I used examples of haiku written by Issa to inspire poets to write haiku with compassion and imagination.

When I announced that I was writing this book, sixty poets contributed their haiku to be included in it as examples: poets from mainly the USA but also from Canada, Europe, and South America. Many contemporary haiku poets still find inspiration in the work of Edo-period Issa.

How can this be?

One possible reason for Issa's lasting popularity and continuing ability to inspire is his compassion, what he would have labeled, *ninjou*. He cares about orphan sparrows and beggar children because he sees *himself* in them. For today's world of hate, violence, immigrant-loathing, and existential loneliness within impersonal, densely populated cities, Issa's ability to identify with, and show empathy for, other beings is perhaps an important lesson.

There are some poets and scholars, however, who disapprove of what they call 'sentimentality' in Issa's haiku. One prominent critic of Japanese literature, Earl Miner, for example, sees Issa as being too focused on subjective experience and personal feeling to be ranked among the great haiku masters, such as Issa's role model, Bashō (*The Princeton Companion to Classical Japanese Literature* 94). Such critics expect more detachment, more distance between poet and what the poet is portraying. They appreciate the fact that Bashō tends to keep a wall, albeit a thin one, between himself and what he observes, evident in a famous haiku written about a night spent at an inn:-

一家に遊女も寝たり萩と月
hitotsu ie ni asobime mo netari hagi to tsuki

95

at an inn
where hookers sleep too
bush clover and the moon

Even though, according to his journal, he could hear through the wall the two prostitutes talking to each other, Bashō maintains objective distance: he is the moon, shining coldly above the earthbound, passionate 'flowers'. Issa, in contrast, tends to write himself into poetic scenes as an involved presence. In doing so, he is applying a completely modern insight. The 'observer effect' in modern physics is a theory that states that the act of observing an event or phenomenon inevitably changes it. Here's one example of the kind of haiku that Professor Miner disdained but that I believe not only manifests but celebrates the 'observer effect'.

痩蛙まけるな一茶是に有り

yasegaeru makeru-na issa kore ni ari

scrawny frog, hang tough!
Issa
is here

When I first read this haiku, I imagined that Issa was offering to jump into the pond to help the skinny frog with physical force, but a Japanese advisor, Keizo Kuramoto, convinced me that he is most likely only encouraging the frog. Issa identifies with it. His life, too, is hard, but he's not giving up; he keeps struggling. When he says *issa kore ni ari* ('Issa is here') he is saying, 'I am with you; I feel for you; don't give up the fight. *Ganbatte!*' The so-called 'subjectivity' in Issa isn't romantic self-indulgence. It is an honest – what we might call today, postmodern – admission that there's no real separation between self and other, observer and observed. In a similar vein, when he urges a flea to jump on to a lotus blossom, a Buddhist symbol for enlightenment, he is just as surely encouraging himself (and us) to do so:-

蚤飛べよおなじ事なら蓮の上

nomi tobe yo onaji koto nara hasu no ue

jump flea!
might as well be
onto a lotus

96

To borrow a line from Lennon and McCartney, 'your inside is out, and your outside is in'. By maintaining an awareness of inextricable connection and interdependence with others – other people, other life forms – Issa's poetic approach serves well in 2019 (which, incidentally, happens to be exactly two hundred years after he wrote the 'jump flea!' haiku).

Issa's compassion for animals is legendary. Another typical example follows:-

こほろぎの寒宿とする衾哉

kourogi no kanshuku to suru fusuma kana

> the cricket's
> winter residence...
> my quilt

Issa welcomes the cricket that has come to visit his bedding on a cold winter night as a roommate rather than as a pest. He acknowledges the life and sentience of his small visitor: the night is just as cold for a cricket as it is for a man. The world, for Issa, is a commonly shared space wherein a man and a cricket can enjoy a bed's comforting warmth on a winter's night. This perspective, born of the Buddhism that Issa fervently practiced, happens to have become a popular view among ecologically-minded earthlings of the 21st century. Again, Issa, though living in the Edo period, espoused a quite contemporary idea. One of the contributors to *Write like Issa*, Deborah P Kolodji, consciously follows his example when she writes:-

> one ant circles
> the toilet rim
> new roommate   (*Write like Issa* 15)

Gregory Piko, another of the contributors to *Write like Issa*, understands, as did Issa, that it's perfectly OK to present one's subjective experience in a haiku and to mingle it with the perceptions and reality of a bird:-

> a finch in the sun
> I am well
> after all   (*Write like Issa* 71)

97

Issa didn't hesitate to write about his personal struggles and sorrows in his haiku. In this way he anticipates 20th and 21st century neuro-scientists and phenomenologists who have shown that our so-called 'reality' is actually a construct of individual and group consciousness. To leave one's self out of the picture is to show only half of the picture. A young poet in my haiku group in New Orleans, Nicholas M Sola (who last year edited the members' anthology for the Haiku Society of America – and did a terrific job), boldly tells his deeply personal truth in this next haiku.

first blossoms –
he identifies
as bisexual   (*Write like Issa* 75)

Nicholas, like Issa, refuses to self-censor. His own reality, his own consciousness – including his own sexual identity – are as much a part of the universe as are the first blossoms of spring.

One of my favorite haiku poets in the world is Petar Tchouhov of Bulgaria. He contributed several haiku to the *Write like Issa* book, including this one.

night storm
I'm thinking about
the dolls in the attic   (*Write like Issa* 23)

Tchouhov establishes a feeling of profound existential loneliness in a vast, indifferent universe. During the night storm he is thinking about – not a fellow human being – but, surprisingly, dolls confined in the attic. Might they symbolically represent his own forever-lost, locked up, and shut away childhood? Like Issa, we deeply sense a human being's most intimate reality in this haiku. Tchouhov thinks about the mysterious dolls while thunder crashes in the night. We think about the dolls, too: his dolls, and ours.

When Rick Clark writes the following haiku about a cabbage butterfly – a small, white butterfly found in Great Britain and New Zealand – he expresses Issa-like empathy – which is evidently why he contributed this verse to the book:-

border crossing—
a cabbage butterfly flits
from daisy to daisy   (*Write like Issa* 26)

The butterfly can fly freely, blissfully unconscious of the human construct of a border. Without breathing a word about the injustice of a rich nation slamming shut its iron door to the poor, the destitute, and the politically oppressed of other lands; Clark implies all this. The butterfly seeks daisies, and people at the border seek a better life. Europe, the United States, South America – the whole world, it seems these days, is grappling with the problem of borders. Issa's example is painfully contemporary. He writes:-

牢屋から出たり入つたり雀の子
rouya kara detari ittari suzume no ko

> in and out
> of prison it goes...
> baby sparrow

Issa's baby sparrow (or perhaps many baby sparrows) flies easily and innocently back and forth between the carefully demarcated human realms of 'prison' and 'freedom'. Such categories, of course, mean nothing to it. In their poems, Clark and Issa challenge their readers to contemplate the suffering that borders and prisons can cause.

Another lesson that Issa can teach poets of today is to open themselves more completely to life's experiences: to see, hear, touch, smell, taste, and – deeply – feel.

牛もうもうもうと霧から出たりけり
ushi mou mou mou to kiri kara detari keri

> moo, moo, moo
> from fog the cows
> emerge

Here, sound transmogrifies into solid entities: cows emerging from an autumn fog. Issa's life-lesson here – actually a quite ancient one that the

Taoists of old China accepted as a matter of course but that human begins in our industrialized, technological age sorely need to learn – is simply to stop, look, and listen: open the floodgates of sense and heart, and contemplate the sheer wonder of it all.

Another example from Nicholas M Sola is quite Issa-like in this respect.

> spring forest—
> all the colors
> of socks   (*Write like Issa* 34)

Achieving childlike vision, as Nicholas manages to do here, is actually quite a difficult task, analogous to Pablo Picasso's artistic evolution from 'grown-up' realism to colorful and whimsical creations that sing of an inner child set free. The adult mind compartmentalizes: forests and socks occupy distinct and separate realms of experience in such a mind. The child's mind, however, combines and blurs: so many colors in these woods, so many socks! The connection isn't logical (the purview of adult thinking) but magical. Nicholas opens himself to wonder and to magic, here and now, and this marvellous haiku results.

Issa did not hesitate to use his imagination in his haiku. For example, he wrote four haiku about a *daibutsu*'s (that is, a Great Buddh statue's) nose, from 1813 to 1822. Since he wrote these poems in Shinano Province, far away from the famous Great Buddha statues of Nara and Kamakura, he must have relied on either memory or imagination to compose the first one: in it, he hears baby sparrows chirping inside a hollow, great bronze Buddha's nose. In the second one he envisions morning fog escaping from the nose. In the third he sees the soot of a soot-sweeper fall from it. Finally, in 1822, he writes:

大仏の鼻から出たる乙鳥哉
daibutsu no hana kara detaru tsubame kana

> from the great bronze
> Buddha's nose...
> a swallow!

By restlessly revising – trying out new combinations of remembered experiences – Issa ultimately arrives at his masterpiece poem in which the Great Buddha sneezes forth... a swallow!

Contemporary poet Michael Dylan Welch submitted this haiku for *Write like Issa.*

> sun through the rain . . .
> a fox is getting married
> in my dream   (*Write like Issa* 81)

The haiku is very surrealistic, very *gendai* – but Michael is simply following the example of Edo-period Issa. He dares to use his imagination to create scenes that are *based on* objective reality but not *found there*. In this way he expresses his inner truth.

This is also the poetic approach of British poet Stuart Bartow, who contributed this haiku to the book:

> summer's bees
> frozen
> into winter stars   (*Write like Issa* 84)

Imagination penetrates experience to extract a truth deeper than the literal. Issa's swallows materialize like a miraculous sneeze from the Universal Buddha, intimating a truth about life: we have all been thrown here – into the light – for a brief, flashing moment, heading to who-knows-where? And Stuart Bartow's bees metamorphose into frozen stars not literally but through an exercise of imagination that, Issa-like, hints of life's Big Picture: from hot, buzzing life to cold, silent, eternity. Stuart, like Issa, dares to go beyond the mere description of reality to explore its deeper connections and non-logical truths.

Another well-known characteristic of Issa is his humor which saturates thousands of his haiku. Comedy arises from incongruity: in the following haiku there's the incongruity of an important official performing a humbling but necessary biological task. There is also, of course, a hint of social satire in the verse, suggesting that even high-ranking members of society are, under their robes of authority, just like everyone else.

春風や大宮人の野雪隠

haru kaze ya oumiyabito no no setchin

spring breeze –
the great courtier
poops in the field

Elliot Nicely, like Issa, finds humor in bodily functions.

constipated—
the long echo
of a train's horn   (*Write like Issa* 54)

Constipation certainly ranks far below cherry blossoms on a list of the most common topics for haiku. This is one source of the poem's humor: its opening image constitutes a jarring surprise in relation to ordinary topics of haiku poetry. From this initial surprise, Nicely shifts (nicely) to a second surprise: the sound of 'the long echo/of a train's horn'. Nicely leaves plenty of space for the reader's imagination to work. I choose to picture the poor, constipated subject of the poem staying up late at night in a bathroom, straining without success until – instead of physical relief – the only 'blast' in the night is that of a distant train horn. The poem is funny in the way that Issa's poems (like that of the pooping courtier) are funny: we laugh but we also accept the poet's invitation to commiserate and contemplate.

In many countries children blow the seeds of dandelions to make wishes. In this next example by Greg Longenecker, there are no children in the scene.

abandoned farm
the dandelions make
their own wishes   (*Write like Issa* 58)

With no one around, especially no children, there's no one to blow the dandelion seeds and make wishes. Instead, Longenecker claims, 'the dandelions make/their own wishes'. This image raises a smile, but the scene of abandoned property with dandelion puff-seeds scattering without human help – blown by a random wind – makes our smile a sad one. The family is absent, hinting that they have lost their farm; they

102

couldn't make it work; *their* wishes went unanswered. As with all fine haiku, the most important part of the poem isn't stated outright but gently implied. Issa's humor is often directed at the shortcomings of the human world, which means poets of the twenty-first century have plenty of material with which to emulate him. Issa's attitude, worthy of imitation, might be described: 'Let's laugh at this together, because the alternative is to weep'.

The final chapter of *Write like Issa* shows that some poets today are imitating specific haiku by Issa to create interesting effects. I'll close with one interesting example of this. Issa wrote:

かたつぶりそろそろ登れ富士の山
katatsuburi soro-soro nobore fuji no yama

> little snail
> inch by inch, climb...
> Mount Fuji

And Petar Tchouhov answers Issa with this:-

> so far away
> from Mount Fuji –
> a dead snail   (*Write like Issa* 90)

Tchouhov's answer-poem far transcends humorous parody. In it, he conjures a memory of Issa's original haiku, hence a memory of its original, spiritual message of slow, patient progress moving toward a lofty goal. Mount Fuji, sacred in Shinto, came to represent transcendence to a higher reality in Buddhism. Tchouhov superimposes the memory of Issa's original poem and its optimistic, spiritual implications over a shockingly different presentation of a snail and a mountain. One is dead; the other is 'far away'. There's no enlightenment here, no spiritual advancement. Dark in its implications, Tchouhov's poem is a masterful – and painfully modern – response to Issa. The over twenty-thousand haiku written by Issa are a treasure trove of inspiration for new haiku. As I point out in the book, many of these haiku themselves are response poems to earlier work by Bashō and ancient Chinese poets. Answering

Issa's haiku with our own in a way to contribute to a long and fascinating chain letter.

Writing like Issa requires compassion, an intelligent awareness of the connections among all creatures, an insightful awareness that there is no such thing as 'objective' reality – that one's self is always a part of the poetic equation – a flexible imagination, and a deep, knowing humor. And, on top of that, answering Issa's haiku with our own can be a door to insight and much fun. In all of these ways, Issa, a great poet of the Edo period, appears today as remarkably *gendai*, surprisingly contemporary: an inspiring example for 21st-century haiku poets.

Xavier University of Louisiana

A SENSE OF PLACE
Haiku, Glass and the British Coast

Ian Storr

This project started effectively in 2013. Much as I would like this to be a retrospective, it's more a report of work to date. At this stage of the project's life it is changing fast and I have already had to make several changes to this presentation to accommodate new developments. The project is multidisciplinary, science, poetry and visual art, so it does fit the overall theme of the conference. The three partners come from very different backgrounds.

The story starts with Ric Van Noort, Emeritus Professor in the School of Dentistry at the University of Sheffield and a materials scientist. Glass is one of the materials, used to make dental crowns and sand is an ingredient of glass. For cosmetic purposes, the glass needs to be colourless with pigments added in to match the patient's teeth. This requirement means that only certain sorts of sand can be used. One day, sat on the beach at Southwold, Ric began to wonder what glass would look like if made from the sand around him. So, being a curious scientist, he collected some sand and took it into the Dental Department.

Other ingredients, as well as sand, are used in glass-making: potassium carbonate, sodium carbonate, calcium carbonate and aluminium oxide. The different ingredients are weighed out, mixed together, placed in a crucible, put into a furnace at 1400 degrees centigrade for 3 hours, then poured into a mold and allowed to cool. The Southwold sand made a pale blue glass. The next one, from Whitby, was a very dark brown. Ric was intrigued at the difference. Over the following years, he made a number of glasses, currently somewhere between 40 and 50. These have produced an interesting colour palette.

For display purposes, samples of the sand have also been collected. These differ in colour and texture.

106

The different colours of the glasses are probably generated by different isotopes of iron. There seems to be some correlation between particular geological strata and colour, but it's not predictable. The geology of Great Britain is complex and sand deposits are also affected by tidal patterns.

I was aware of Ric's work through our friendship and fascinated by it. I liked the variety and unpredictability of what he was involved in and the connection with the deep time of geological processes. I wondered about the parallels that could be made between the creation of glass and light from sand and the creation of poetry and space for reflection from the nitty gritty of experience. How different is Ric's AHA! moment on Southwold beach from moments of haiku inspiration? Both can come from an idling but receptive mind. I suggested that Ric's work could be combined with haiku to create a joint work focused on the British coast. He needed some convincing, knowing something but not a lot about haiku. It took me about a year, on and off, but eventually he agreed. The intervention of a mutual friend, involved in arts consultancy, proved crucial. The following were our initial aims: provide different per- spectives on the British Coast and encourage people to reflect on their own experiences of it; bring together scientific and poetic approaches to the same subject; introduce haiku to a wider audience.

It seemed to me that Ric was involved among other things in a mapping exercise and that haiku could provide another dimension to this. One definition of the verb 'map' from *The Shorter Oxford Dictionary* is to: '...establish the relative positions, or the spatial relations or distribution, of (an object or its components)...'

Mapping is about relationships and has a spatial dimension. I would go further and argue that the spatial dimension is the primary organising principle. Haiku would add to Ric's glasses sensory impressions, the dimension of time and, potentially, emotional and spiritual experiences. I would argue that when a number of haiku are related to a particular locality (or in the case of the project a type of locality), this produces a poetic collage that enriches our understanding and experience of the place in question. I'd like to illustrate this using three examples of mapping in haiku and haiku-related forms.

Example 1. Renga – Alec Finlay's *white peak/dark peak* project

I had become interested in mapping with my involvement in 2013 with Alec Finlay's white peak/dark peak project. Working in partnership with other poets, Alec used 20-link renga to focus on and evoke particular walks in the Peak District National Park. These were then brought together to create an on-line audio-visual word map of the whole of the Peak District National Park. Finlay's individual renga are geographically very limited but bring together a wide range of associations with the place concerned. Here are two short extracts from a renga he and I composed on Derwent Edge and Ladybower.

> a shooting butt skyline
> empty on the moonlit moor
>
> blue winter coated
> at the last moment
> the hare jinks away
>
> t'owd landlord at t'Ladybower
> took his whisky in milk
>
> dusk on Brogging Moss
> grouse chuckle
> on a bitter wind
>
> and
>
> the bombers' practice runs
> the length of the reservoir
>
> this battlefield
> where two kings fought
> covered with hoar frost
>
> the first fishermen
> cast in the dawn light

> a black plastic bag
> caught on hawthorn
> flaps in the slipstream of cars

We build up a picture of a specific locality, over space and time, that in these eight links includes the natural history and leisure economy of the Peak, recent and ancient history, two place names and a local character.

Example 2 Haibun – Bashō's *Narrow Road to the Deep North*

The spatial dimension to Bashō's *The Narrow Road to the Deep North*, is clear. The prose is the account of an actual journey to the North of Japan, which can be traced on a map. For Bashō this journey was organised around poetic places (*utamakura*), particularly temples, shrines and famous natural features, places with stories attached to them. He was very mindful of his poetic predecessors, particularly the waka poet Saigyō. He used this poetic legacy to make himself more receptive to the places he was visiting but he was also very conscious of adding to the legacy. As well as adding to the poetic culture of Japan, Bashō was also undertaking a spiritual journey. He was aware of his own ageing at the outset. Just after the visit to Ashino, when he came to the Barrier gate of Shirakawa, he described himself in these words: 'Here, for the first time, my mind was able to gain a certain balance and composure, no longer a victim to pestering anxiety'. The visits to temples and shrines were at least part pilgrimage. Awe and compassion are frequent responses to his experiences of particular places. These themes are illustrated in the following three haiku:-

> over an entire field
> they have planted rice – before
> I part with the willow
> > *Translation by Makoto Ueda*

The willow tree is the one Saigyō wrote his famous waka about. It was still there in Bashō's time by a rice field in Ashino village. Like Saigyō before him Bashō lingered by the tree, the poem implies, lost in reverie. Bashō, as he often does, brings together high culture and the everyday, in this case Saigyō's waka and the workers in the field.

109

the rough sea –
flowing towards Sado Isle
the River of Heaven
Translation by Makoto Ueda

Sado, an island in the Sea of Japan, was known for its many sad stories of prisoners exiled there. Perhaps the rough sea for Bashō evoked the hard fates dealt to the exiles, but the overwhelming feeling is of a lonely grandeur.

summer grasses –
traces of dreams
of ancient warriors
Translation by Haruo Shirane

Bashō describes himself as weeping at the ancient battlefield where three generations of the Fujiwara family perished. There is an unstated compassion in the poem, alongside the recognition of the transience of life.

Example 3 Haiku – Wally Swist

For decades Wally Swist has written haiku in the area around Amherst, Massachusetts. In an interview published in *muttering thunder 1*, he states: 'Sense of place is the core of my life and my poetry. The rolling waves of mist and fog that would cross Haskins' Flats at dawn or at dusk still distil and rise within me. Mount Toby is my own spiritual mountain... The outer landscape informs the inner landscape... It is in that interaction that the ego falls away and the best haiku are written.' Walking out into landscape becomes a meditation. It is important to Swist, as it is to other nature poets to know the names of things. He quotes with approval Gary Snyder in Turtle Mountain: 'Learn the flowers/go light'. Swist comments: 'That's it, right there'. Here are some examples of his Amherst haiku that have appeared in *Presence*.

ah, snow geese –
a mated pair; their reflections
rowing in the river

morning after rain...
cedar waxwings rustling
in the honeysuckle

wild meadow
buttercupped before the mountain...
asway with timothy

Note the spatial markers: meadow, mountain and river and the range of life depicted. Over literally hundreds of poems a detailed picture emerges of the natural history of that part of Massachusetts over the four seasons. Underlying it is the poet's emotional and spiritual response to the landscape he has sought out.

These three examples, Finlay, Bashō, Swist, suggest that when haiku are used to map a defined area, the following other dimensions are potentially present, enriching the overall picture:-

* Topographical (e.g. cliff, beach, harbour, estuary)
* Ecological (flora and fauna)
* Temporal (historical, seasonal, time of day)
* Cultural (high and broad)
* Spiritual

It's time now to turn back to the project. In 2113, I advertised for haiku in the *BHS Brief* and *Presence*. Previous publication was a prerequisite. This was a way of managing volume. 42 poets submitted a total of 352 haiku from which we chose 20. We were looking for a variety of subjects and no more than one haiku per site and from any individual poet. The purpose was to get as wide a geographical a spread and range of perspectives as possible. The following are a small sample of those accepted:

Loch Coruisk:
rock, seal and sea
each its own grey
Martin Lucas, Loch Coruisk, Skye

111

Here topographical, ecological and spiritual dimensions are present. Loch Coruisk is a freshwater loch, which is ringed by the mountains of the Black Cuillin and discharges into a sea loch. The naming of the location in the haiku and the presence of the seal conveys a strong sense of the wildness of the scene. The spiritual dimension of the haiku is in the wonder it conveys, and the recognition of underlying connectedness.

> Abbey ruins
> through glassless windows
> strands of cloud from the sea
> *Ian Storr, Whitby*

This is perhaps the one utamakura in the set of 20 haiku. The dimensions are topological (the abbey and the sea) temporal/historical and spiritual with some cultural (literary) associations. The first abbey of Whitby was founded in the seventh century by the king of Northumbria, although the ruins referred to in the poem are those of the 13th century Benedictine foundation. The abbey is an important historical and cultural site. There are strong associations with St Hilda, the first abbess, and with the first English poet, Cædmon. More recently, fans of horror will know the headland on which the abbey is sited as the place Count Dracula came ashore. This haiku sets a sense of the transience of human affairs against the enduring but changing presence of the sea.

> Rainbow's end –
> the crabbing child
> empties her pot
> *Helen Buckingham, Whitstable*

The dimensions here are topological, ecological, temporal and spiritual. The crabs represent the ecological dimension and also site the poem topologically on the sea shore, probably a beach. The ending of the girl's activity, and the rainbow's end combine to suggest that this is, perhaps, the end of the day and, more obliquely, that childhood too comes to an end. The spiritual dimension is in the rainbow as a link between heaven and earth, the backdrop to a child totally absorbed in her activity, now returning the crabs to their proper environment. All these dimensions intersect in this eight word poem, finely balanced between transience and wonder.

112

Ric and I discussed various ideas of how to bring the project to fruition and realised after a while that we needed some help with this. Neither of us are visual artists and we needed this perspective. In December 2015 we approached Kirsty Aubrey, principal lecturer at the Manchester School of Art and much exhibited artist in glass. Ric and I met with Kirsty in early 2016 and briefed her about the project so far. We were clear with her that we were placing no constraints on her work and that she was free to take it where she wanted.

We set about raising funding. We obtained grants from *The British Haiku Society* (October 2017) and *Presence* (January 2018) and an Undergraduate bursary (June 2018). The *BHS* and *Presence* funding was initially to enable us to buy Kirsty out of teaching commitments, but we were given flexibility by both in how we used the money. The undergraduate bursary was primarily used to develop a website. In March 2019 Kirsty's managers agreed that she could spend ten days work time on the project. In April 2019 we obtained funding for filming. The aim of this was to submit two films to *The Crafts Council Film Festival* and *The International Film Festival for Fine Crafts* (FIFMA). In May 2019 a photography student was tasked to produce a zine of the project.

Kirsty's initial thoughts to producing grasses with the beach glass providing the seed heads as in the clip. She had produced an installation along these lines at Walkden Japanese garden in Manchester. However the beach glass was unpredictable – the glass in some samples heated up unevenly and in one instance exploded. There was also a tendency to devitrify. Devitrification can occurs in the firing process where the glass develops crazing or wrinkles as the molecules in the glass change their structure into that of crystalline solids.

Kirsty then looked at producing pieces from moulds. However, Kirsty's research managers at the MSA raised intellectual property issues about the creation of pieces incorporating haiku. Including the haiku within the glass brings up issues of authorship. The glasswork is one person's, the text is someone else's and authorship and ownership becomes too complex. An agreement was reached between Kirsty and her managers to the effect that her work was to focus on visual perceptions of the coast, which led to her work on lenses. The three of us felt that this could both stand alone and also work with the other elements of the project. It is planned to use some of the lenses in conjunction with beach telescopes which Kirsty is currently trying to source. Kirsty is also exploring inscribing other one-line haiku on to some lenses. Examples of work produced so far are included below.

Additional work is well advanced. Work has started on the zine (= publication in magazine form). This will bring the various strands of the project together and also serve as publicity and promotional material. The *BHS* and *Presence* funding will support the production and publication costs of this. The following are examples of possible inserts.

114

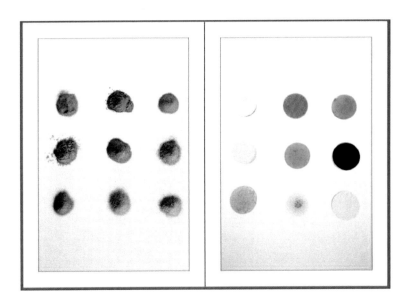

waiting together
for the right tide-
surfers and resting gulls

by *Martha Street*

Gwythin, St Ives

Kirsty has made a successful bid for exhibition space this September at the prestigious *International Association of Societies of Design Research* Conference in Manchester (September 2019) and we are also planning to apply for exhibition space at the *National Glass Centre* in Sunderland in 2020.

Other work being discussed but not being actively pursued at this point in time includes expanding the website; cataloguing the glasses and sands photographically as a resource for the project; and an anthology of coastal haiku. We would need to identify funding for the last. It wouldn't necessarily be a conventional anthology. I would see it also including photographic material from the project and perhaps a short account of it. The excitement of the project has been the twists and turns it has taken and, hopefully, will continue to take in the future when three different people from three different backgrounds embark on a joint venture.

August 2019

NANO-HAIKU:
A Possible Meeting Point between East and West
Antoaneta Nikolova and Yordan M. Georgiev

(Funded by the European Union through the Marie Sklodowska-Curie Action, Horizon 2020, as a part of Antoaneta Nikolova's individual project 'Perception of Eastern Teachings in Europe'. This work was also partially funded by the Strategic Research Fund of University College Cork (UCC), Ireland, the College of Arts and Celtic Studies and Social Sciences Creative Practice Support Fund of UCC under the Nanohaiku Project.)

Introduction

What is haiku? Why does this Far Eastern mode of poetry attract the attention of so many people in the contemporary world? In this paper, we present one unusual approach to these questions, describing haiku as a possible meeting point of East and West, art and science. Using advanced nanofabrication techniques such as Electron Beam Lithography (EBL) and Directed Self-Assembly (DSA) of Block Co-Polymers (BCP) in conjunction with the shortest poetic form, haiku, we demonstrate how modern scientific methods that result from the development of a Western approach to reality could be combined with old Eastern philosophical and poetical interpretations of this reality in an innovative and intriguing way.

Why do we find it possible to combine these approaches? One of the answers is very simple. Being the shortest poetic form known to humanity, haiku is a kind of 'nano' poetry (just a reminder that the nowadays widely used prefix 'nano' is derived from the Greek word ναυος, which means 'dwarf'). Therefore, a natural and straightforward link between haiku and nanofabrication can be seen and haiku can be considered as a great object on which to demonstrate the amazing capabilities of nanofabrication.

The other answer is connected with the philosophy that underlines the vision of haiku. This is the philosophy of non-duality and mutual response.

117

Haiku as a gap in-between realities

Usually, when interpreting haiku in terms of Western categories, we might ask whether haiku is objective or subjective, whether it depicts an external picture or a landscape of the soul, whether it is external or internal, natural or human. The answer to these questions, however, cannot be found in terms of opposing dichotomies that were developed within the Western approach to reality. It should be sought in the Far Eastern understanding of non-duality.

Sometimes haiku looks just like a picture or a description of a story. Sometimes it depicts things as if they were our inner state. Is it a drawing, however, only of the inner or is it to do with the outer landscape? We suggest that haiku is neither only an 'image' of the inner nor only of the outer state, neither only objective nor only subjective.

Haiku is rather an expression of the relation between the inner and the outer, in which they are not distinguished anymore. The invisible relationship, indicated mostly with a dash or simply by absence or emptyness, is what haiku expresses and leads to. Haiku is entering through the gap of the relation into the deepest levels of the processing ontology, where there is neither being nor non-being, but only possibilities for becomings and unfoldings.

Haiku is an example of poetry written from the position of the centre within the circle of changes, which is also the ever-new centre of the creative happening. It is entering into the gap between two realities or levels of reality that are not isolated entities but reflections and echoes vibrating in their changeability, from one side, and reaching the thread of the axis that might connect or divide them from the other.

In Daoism, the centre within the circle of changes is called the pivot of dao, 'the axis of motion'. Interestingly, the Chinese character, which we translate as a pivot, means a door hinge – i.e., this is the axis that allows transition and entry into a new state. In this sense, the pivot is also a threshold, that is, emptiness opened to something that is about to unfold, emptiness that you can get through. This is the area of endless possibilities at the centre of the world circle, where the events are yet to come and the potential for their realisation is inexhaustible:-

118

When that and this both fail to get their counterpart, we have what is called the pivot point of the Dao. The pivot gets placed at the centre of the circle in order to respond to the infinite. Affirmations involve an infinity, and denials also involve an infinity. Therefore it is said: 'There is nothing like brightness'. (Zhuangzi, 2)

The achievement of this pivot can be interpreted in both the epistemological and ontological sense. On the one hand, it is the insight of the mutuality of opposites *'this* is also *that,* and *that* is also this *'*, where any affirmation is also a denial, and vice versa. This, however, is also a pre-potential state from which all possibilities and un-possibilities spring, this is the state of flexibility and openness to all states, events and processes.

Haiku, as well as every true poetry, reaches exactly this pivot at the centre of changes, which is a pure potentiality, where the actualisation of possibilities is yet to come. From this position any links between future unfoldings are possible. Therefore poetry, and every real creativity as well, is able to connect seemingly impossible things, and it does it in an effortless and natural way. When the link between things is made from this level, it is perceived as completely natural, however strange, unknown or unexpected it might be.

This naturalness of links is a sign of the true poetry. When the centre of unfoldings is not reached, the connections are violent and artificial, they might provoke our intellectual admiration, but they do not resonate within us.

For Eastern thought, this centre is not some transcendent extreme to be achieved. Every concrete thing or event can lead us to it. It is at the heart of every process and can be reached from anywhere.

It is not accidental that haiku should be concrete. For Far-Eastern thought, it is exactly through the concrete that universal is attained, and the universal is manifested only through and in what is concrete.

With its brevity, haiku represents precisely such compressed break-through to the centre, from which the unfoldings are immense.

This is clearly visible in its form, where what's important is the empty, unspoken space or state between two different perspectives or positions (in time, space, thought, etc.).

So, haiku enters into the gap in-between, where there is no subject nor object but only mutually echoing relations.

Contemporary science, however, also penetrates into the depth of the reality into those underlying states where the manifestation of the visible world is about to be manifested.

What will happen if we put the form of haiku into these levels? In order to answer this question we used some methods of contemporary science.

Nanofabrication

Nanofabrication is an approach that is widely used in high-tech research and development (R&D) as well as in the microelectronics technology. It encompasses a large variety of processes and methods for creating structures and devices with minimum dimensions lower than 100 nm (nm – nanometre – one billionth, 10^{-9}, of a meter), which have a vast range of applications. Just one comparison here – the human hair has a thickness of about 100 μm (micrometre), which is 100,000 nm, i.e. it is 1000 to 100,000 times larger than the structures that are the subject of nanofabrication.

Among all the processes and methods of nanofabrication, electron beam lithography (EBL) and directed self-assembly (DSA) of block co-polymer (BCP) techniques are becoming increasingly widespread in research and development as a potential application for scaling down semiconductor device patterning. EBL, especially, is by far the most widely used nanofabrication technique in R&D because of its flexibility, maturity and very high resolution. The EBL process is very similar to the much more popular photography with the main difference that instead of light, EBL uses a finely focussed beam of fast electrons to write the required pattern in a thin sacrificial layer called 'resist', which is deposited on the main working material (see figure 1). The electron beam resembles an extremely fine pencil with a 'tip' of 2-3 nm, which is, however, controlled not manually but automatically by a computer.

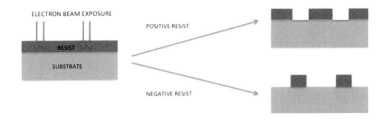

Figure 1. Schematic presentation of the process of electron beam lithography

As a result of the exposure of the resist with electrons, its properties change locally. Subsequent 'development' in a suitable 'developer' either dissolves the exposed sites of the resist (positive resist) or the unexposed sites (negative resist). This creates a mask (stencil) through which the 'active' material of the substrate can then be locally processed. This is done either by removing parts of this material by 'etching' or by locally adding other material. It is worth noting that EBL has an extremely high resolution – it is capable of creating structures with dimensions of only a few nanometres (10-15 atoms!).

The second method mentioned above is the DSA of BCP (BCP is a polymeric material composed of two different co-polymers). This process is relatively new and has since recently been used for a new type of high-resolution lithography with potentially high throughput, called DSA or BCP lithography. Here, instead of the resist as in EBL, a thin layer of BCP is spin-coated on the substrate. During a particular treatment of this layer (usually thermal treatment), processes of self-organisation and 'phase separation' occur in it, in which the two co-polymers separate from each other. Subsequently, one of the co-polymers can be removed with a suitable solvent, thereby forming with the other co-polymer a spontaneous image that most often resembles a fingerprint and in some cases is in the form of vertical cylinders.

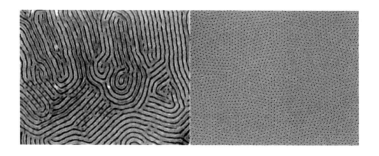

Figure 2. *Two spontaneous BCP images taken with a scanning electron microscope (SEM): one resembling a fingerprint and the other in the form of vertical cylinders. The size of the lines and dots in the two images is about 20 nm.*

The patterns shown in figure 2 are obtained when the block co-polymers are spin-coated on a smooth surface. However, if there are any pre-formed structures on the surface of the substrate, the block co-polymers experience their disturbing, limiting or directing influence during the processes of self-organization and phase separation. Thus, the block co-polymers form patterns that are shaped by the form and size (geometry) of the structures present on the surface. This process of 'directed self-assembly' has recently been used very intensively to produce BCP images of a particular shape that can have wide technological application (see figure 3).

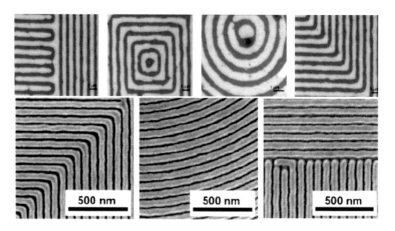

Figure 3. *Selection of SEM images of ordered structures created using DSA of BCP.*

122

Nanofabrication, haiku and haiga: nanohaiku and nanohaiga

After briefly presenting the two nanofabrication methods, we are going to discuss how we used them to create nano-sized haiku and haiga. It is worth mentioning here that *haiga* is a combination of a haiku with a painting inspired by the haiku itself. Usually the painting is not merely an illustration to the haiku but, according to the Eastern principle of mutual response, it complements and enriches haiku's suggestion.

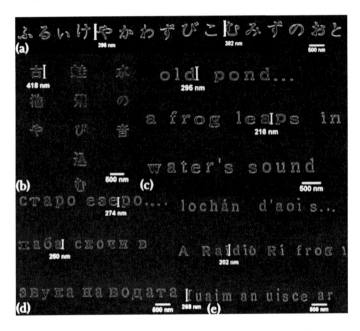

Figure 4. SEM micrographs of nano-versions of the haiku poem 'The old pond' by Matsuo Bashō. The poem is written by EBL with the HSQ resist on Si substrates in five languages and four different alphabets/character styles: (a) contemporary Japanese, (b) classical Japanese, (c) English, (d) Bulgarian and (e) Irish. The size of the whole letters/characters is between 200-400 nm but the width of the lines outlining them is down to 20 nm.

Thus, EBL and the hydrogen silsesquioxane (HSQ) negative tone electron resist were used for capturing on silicon (Si) substrates (Si is the most widely used material in microelectronics) nanoscale examples of the tiniest haiku poems written in six languages having four different

123

character styles/alphabets (Japanese, English, Bulgarian, Irish, Danish and Marathi). Here, beside one of the most famous haiku 'The old pond' by Matsuo Bashō, haiku poems written by Bulgarian, Irish and Indian authors were used as well. The nanoscale haiku poems (*'nanohaiku'*) written by EBL on Si substrates were inspected by a high-resolution scanning electron microscopy (SEM). The SEM images show that the size of the haiku texts (letters/characters) varies from around 200 nm for the simpler Cyrillic and Latin letters to the range of 400-800 nm for the more complex Chinese, Japanese and Marathi characters (see figures 4 and 5). However, the width of the lines outlining each individual letter/character is down to 20 nm and even below, which is very close to the limit of the EBL technology. To the best of our knowledge, these nanoscale haiku poems are the smallest haiku ever written until now.

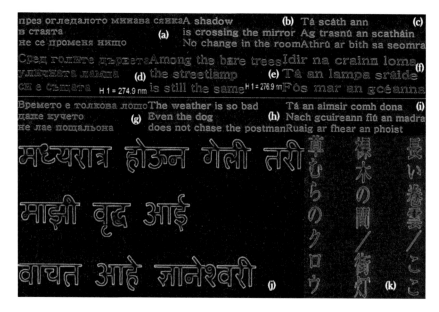

Figure 5. SEM micrographs of nano-versions of haiku poems by the authors, (a)-(f), written on Si substrates by EBL with the HSQ resist in Bulgarian (left), English (middle) and Irish (right) columns: (a)-(c) AN and (d)-(f) YMG; (g)-(i) haiku written by Nedyalka Panova. Image (j) shows a haiku poem by Shri Bal Rane written in Marathi and (k) presents the first phrases of three haiku poems written by YMG and translated in Japanese [7]. The size of the whole Latin and Cyrillic letters is in the range 200-300 nm, whereas the size of the Marathi, Chinese and Japanese characters is between 500-800 nm. The width of the smallest lines outlining the letters/characters, however, is down to 20 nm.

124

Furthermore, DSA of BCP was used in conjunction with the EBL process. DSA is a method, which employs pre-written guiding structures to organise BCPs in such a way as to form precise nanostructures with certain shapes that may have many applications. In our case the 'nanohaiku' poems similar to the ones shown in figures 4 and 5 were used as guiding features between which a thin film (ca. 50 nm thick) of a specific block co-polymer was spin coated to create self-organised nanopatterns. After the spin coating, a thermal annealing was done in toluene solvent vapours at 50 °C for 1.5 hours to phase-separate the two copolymers and then the Si samples were immersed in ethanol for 15 hours at 40 °C to dissolve one of the co-polymers and improve the visual contrast of the obtained patterns. Finally, the resulting EBL and BCP structures (*nanohaiku* and *nanohaiga*) were inspected by high-resolution SEM.

It was interesting to discover how the matter, in this case block co-polymers, will spontaneously react to the very structure of the haiku poems written at a nanoscale and what pictures would these interactions reveal. Thus, the idea of this experiment is to investigate the 'response' of the block co-polymers to the geometry and meaning of nanostructured haiku written in different languages with very different topography, which is expected to lead to the possible emergence of spontaneous '*nanohaiga*' around the *nanohaiku* poems.

Figure 6 on page 126 demonstrates examples of structures formed in and around more complex individual Chinese characters (figures 6a-c) from haiku poems by Yordan M. Georgiev translated into Japanese as well as in and around Cyrillic letters and phrases from haiku poems written in Bulgarian by Antoaneta Nikolova (figure 6d) and Nedyalka Panova (figure 6e). It is well seen that within the characters the BCP forms straight or curved horizontal lines with periodicity of ~40 nm, which follow the shape of the characters. In contrast, outside the characters and the poems as a whole, the predominant structures are vertical cylinders with the same periodicity.

In general, the larger and graphically more complex Chinese, Japanese, and Marathi characters exhibited stronger influence on the self-organisation of the BCP than the smaller and simpler Latin and Cyrillic letters. Therefore, more interesting and attractive BCP structures were observed within and around the Chinese, Japanese, and Marathi characters.

Figure 6. SEM micrographs of sample structures formed in and around: (a-c) complex individual Chinese characters from haiku poems by YMG translated into Japanese and (d-e) Cyrillic letters and phrases from haiku poems written in Bulgarian by AN (d) and NP (e), all written on Si by EBL using the HSQ resist.

Unfortunately, to image with SEM the whole nanohaiku poems or phrases, a low magnification mode had to be used at which the SEM resolution was not high enough to properly distinguish the tiny BCP structures around the poems. Therefore, we were not able to capture and demonstrate a full-bodied nanohaiga image. Nevertheless, the shown images of single characters and words prove that the BCP does indeed interact with the *nanohaiku* structures and forms unusual patterns around them, which can be interpreted as self- assembled '*nanohaiga*', directed by the morphology and the linguistic geometry of the '*nanohaiku*'. Moreover, they demonstrate how the BCP pattern changes when interacting with the same verse translated into different languages. Thus to the haiku poem's own nanostructure and meaning a new visual identity, '*nanohaiga*', was added combining for the first time poetry, visual art and advanced nanofabrication technologies.

126

The 'nanohaiku' and 'nanohaiga' structures demonstrate in a fascinating way the capabilities of nanofabrication. We believe that thereby these technologies will be made much more appealing and easily accessible both for scientists and lay audience.

Conclusion

As we showed haiku goes to the depth of reality into the level of non-duality and mutual response. Contemporary physics also goes to the deepest levels of reality where form and structure could change the energetic patterns. Combination of Western technologies and Eastern poetry influenced these patterns and resulted in a new form of abstract art at the nanoscale. The form of the written words created a new structure. Did, however, the meaning of these words influence the change? The question is open.

HAIKU IN SCANDINAVIA:
LANGUAGE AND CULTURAL REFERENCE

Anna Maris

Italicised paragraphs represent comments added after the talk by Anna herself.

I write haiku and senryu and renku in English and Swedish. I also teach haiku in schools in Sweden, where I meet mainly people who are between 12 and 16, but sometimes much younger people as well. And it is such a gift to be given, to teach haiku to young people.

I could write a book on teaching haiku to young people (maybe I will!) but one of the most interesting things about it is that they have so much of the 'haiku' spirit through their consumption of Japanese youth culture. It is very easy to explain the haiku elements, including wabi-sabi, karumi, yugen *etc to a young Scandinavian audience, because they have absorbed the Japanese aesthetics, mythology and way of thinking through* anime, *computer games and other Japanese artforms, such as* sashiki *and* origami *already!*

I am also on the board of the Swedish haiku society and I am very much involved with the literary scene in Sweden. The not-haiku literary scene. So I get a lot of questions about the form and often very predictable conversation, such as, "Does it have to be 5-7-5?" ("No!") and, "If it's not 5-7-5 – then what is haiku?" And then I get a question, quite often whether haiku is really poetry. And I say, "Yes!", because if it is not poetry, then it is also not haiku.

How many people have been to a Nordic country – that is Sweden, Denmark, Norway, Finland or Iceland? *(A few!)*

And a second question – how many people have links to a Nordic country? *(Also a few, mainly Swedes and Americans)*

The other day, I was in a debate on digitalization and literature and poetry. And there were lots of people saying that digitalization is a bad thing because you shouldn't read digitally and they use their computers far too much and they don't read books. And I said that if it wasn't for digitalization, I would have an audience of about two people for my poetry, because not very many people are interested in haiku in my country. So I am very grateful for digitalization and it's a total prerequisite for what I do in writing haiku. And I often talk about the international haiku community and say that I have publishers in America and the UK, haiku friends in Japan on Facebook that I have never met (although now I have!)

I'm going to tell you a little bit about the temple where I have a haiku school. It is a Chinese temple in the South of Sweden run by a polish Buddhist monk, who specializes in Traditional Chinese medicine, mainly acupuncture and qi-gong. It's a wonderful place and I invite people to come there and learn about haiku. You are very welcome there. It is a very peaceful place.

The reason for the temple anecdote was to come back to the conference theme – haiku crossing cultures – harmony within diversity.

People very often will ask lots of questions about haiku and I will tell them lots of things and then I will tell them that people all over the world write this form.

Then people often say – "It must be very different the way you write haiku in different countries of the world," and I say, "No, it's not" – and that's a beautiful thing, because it's the way a lone tree bends to the wind or how darkness surrounds the stars, or the fleeting existence of cherry blossoms, or mayflies, or falling leaves. And as people, we are not very different in the observations that we make regardless of where we are in the world. And I find that very touching in these times of polarization and political anxiety and sometimes aggression.

And when I train qi-gong in my temple, my master always says that when we train qi-gong, we connect with all of the other people in the world who are doing qi gong and I have started to do that when I write haiku too, so if you feel an itch or a disturbance… that is why!

Because I think that haiku also has that spirit to move people, to change people collectively somehow. And that is also why ginko is such a powerful thing. But although there are many similarities in haiku between different countries there are of course also differences. If you look at Scandinavian countries, although we don't speak the same language, Swedish, Danish and Norwegian are all quite easily understood, I think anyway, between the different nations, Finnish is a different story. Icelandic and Faeroese becomes a little bit harder, but if you have a trained ear, you can pick it up. So we don't speak the same language but we do understand each other. On the other hand, it is a little bit like America and the UK: you know that saying – two great nations divided by a common language – and sometimes we fall into that trap of thinking, "Oh yes, I know what you mean," when really we are quite different after all...

Scandinavian countries together have quite a few similarities with Japan, which is a curious thing, because it really is on the other side of the world from us, both in geography and in mentality in many ways, we are in many senses polar opposites, on each side of a rainbow, but we have many things in common too. First of all, there is a great affinity with nature and in our old mythology, there is almost a sort of Shintoism, where we attribute spirits to natural elements – or to all elements in a way, although primarily natural elements. In Iceland, for example, they will build a straight road from one end of the island to another, but it won't be straight because you have to build around the spirits that live on certain parts of the stretch. This is still done even though nobody believes in these spirits anymore.

There is also a love for minimalism – Alvar Aalto, the Finnish designer, is very big in Japan – and we very much appreciate that simplicity of a wabi-sabi lifestyle, which Charles mentioned in his talk about Georgia O'Keeffe. And we also have quite a sparse language and not nearly as many synonyms as the English language, because we only have one linguistic line – you have the Latin, the Saxon and lots of other things besides, which makes the English dictionary, depending on how you count, three or four times as large as that of a Scandinavian language. We don't have quite so much room to express ourselves. But this can also be a good thing, as I think that it is the attraction of the limitations that bring us all to the haiku form. We also have something else which is central to our culture, which is central in the old Norse mythology, about stoicism, and dying in battle. I can see great parallels between our Viking culture and that of the Samurai, where honour and also violence, uttering memorable words as we are slain, that brings my thoughts to the death poems of Japan.

There is a quirk in the Scandinavian languages, which we can use very much to our advantage. It is a useful technique that I mentioned very briefly yesterday, when Colin and I were judging the haiku competition and we had the senryu about the lingerie in Marks and Spencers. It is the job of the poet to put into words other people's feelings and capture the contexts that they understand, because otherwise only I would understand the point of my poems and that is pointless, because the point of a poem is to share it. So we have these sown-together words that we can make up as we wish. Autumn rain becomes *höstregn* (autumnrain), when we write it together; you can make up all sorts of words, not just the ones that are in the dictionary, but any word. Recently, one of my students at my temple wrote the word *holköga* in a poem. A *holk* is a birdbox and *öga* means 'eye'. So birdboxeye became a word – that is the creativity in our languages, which is quite appealing – so Northern lights become *norrsken* (lit. 'northshine') and winter sky becomes *vinterhimmel.* I encourage my students to make up and tap into those expressions that people can feel an affinity with, particularly the seasonal ones. We don't have *sajiki* in Sweden, no dictionaries of *kigo*, so we have to make up our own. For example, *midsommarnatt* is 'midsummer-night' in Sweden. I can say that and all Swedish people go weak at the knees. It's the light, it's the smells, it's the sound, it's the music – way in the background – from an old harmonica – it's a whole novel, ultimately, in that one word. The funny thing is that meteorologically speaking, it usually rains in Sweden on midsummer, it is statistically proven that it usually buckets down, but we all know what it *should* be like. And it's a real skill to find these kigo or words that unite our understanding and put words on collective experiences. 'Lingerie in Marks and Spencer's' might be one of those – British people would get a whole spectrum of unified images in a phrase like that.

I personally very much believe in using these common references as a way of identifying national *kigo.* The very function of *kigo* is to 'help the reader' with the season word setting a scene. In non-japanese haiku I think these experiences from nature (or from other contexts) can be used in much the same way, so find ways of triggering your readers!

I would like to invite you to look at the person next to you and talk a little bit about what your *kigo* would be, something from your culture (and pair yourselves with somebody you don't know from a different country to describe your ultimate *kigo*).

British *kigo* might be: seaside (images of beach, icecream, feeling of summer, children playing); midsummer (a much richer experience, rituals of flowers, white nights/midnight sun, a remarkable time of the year).

There is much more to be said on the subject of Scandinavian haiku than the 20 minutes I got to speak allowed for. Sweden has undoubtedly the most well developed haiku scene of all of the Nordic countries. This is because of a long and rich history, which starts already in the 1930's when the Swedish Academy member Anders Österling wrote an essay on Asataro Miyamori's book 'An anthology of haiku ancient and modern' which was published in 1932. Following this, we had a number of early haiku poets, including Bo Setterlind, Dag Hammarskjöld (also general secretary of the UN) and Tomas Tranströmer (who was named a Nobel Laureate of Literature in 2011). Interestingly enough the person who really brought haiku to the mainstream in Sweden was Jan Vintilescu, who wrote an instruction book of haiku in 1959, which did not advocate 5-7-5 syllable count. In other words the Swedes bypassed both Harold Henderson and RH Blyth. Following this, two Swedish ambassadors to Japan, Kaj Falkman and Lars Vargö, have both been instrumental in developing haiku in Sweden and are, in part, the explanation of the very large number of accomplished haiku poets coming out of Sweden. The Swedish haiku society (formed in 1999) have long abandoned a 5-7-5 syllable count and are well versed in the haiku elements through regular workshops, ginko and haiku schools. There around 50 Swedish poets who are part of the international haiku scenes, a remarkable figure for a small country which is not English speaking!

In Denmark, the haiku group is part of the Danish authors' union. They have worked to inspire mainstream authors to also write haiku and are holding firmly on to the 5-7-5 format until this day. The Danish haiku sentiment leans generally much more towards senryu than the other Nordic countries, also to attract a wider appeal, even if many poets also write seasonal haiku. The lighter take on haiku might be a national trait.

Finland has a haiku group which meets regularly in Helsinki, and also advocates a 5-7-5 syllable count, although many of the poems do not follow this pattern. Finnish haiku seems to have two directions, either strictly nature haiku or very experimental short poetry. Finland is a country of contrast, the stereotypical idea of Nordic people is that the further north you get, the more sparse the language gets. But the Finnish are also very passionate people, and are famous for their Finnish tango and their abilities on air guitars. This is, as all stereotypes of course not the whole truth, but no smoke without fire!

Norway and Iceland do not have their own haiku societies but individual poets write haiku in those languages. As there is no local haiku scene, most of the poets gather their inspiration from international sources, very often the old Japanese haiku masters. Poems tend to be more traditional and true to the form, which is also a trait of Norway and Iceland as countries, where history and tradition are very important in society as a whole.

●

The last four paragraphs are largely what I intended to speak about in my talk and I am grateful for the opportunity to present them here.

Anna Maris

Lorca (left) and family 1919

THE TREMBLING OF THE MOMENT   Paul Chambers
The Haiku of Federico García Lorca

As a student in Madrid during the early 1920's, Federico García Lorca discovered the Japanese haiku, a genre then enjoying growing prominence in Hispanic literary circles.

At the same time as Lorca discovered the haiku, he was also deeply immersed in his study of the *copla,* the rural Andalusian folk lyric: a form which 'belongs to no one', which 'floats in the wind like golden thistledown', as he wrote. For Lorca, the catalogue of these primitive lyrics held 'the deepest, most moving songs of our mysterious soul'; and it was in the voices of the poor, gypsy communities of Andalusia that he traced the roots of this *cante jondo,* or 'deep song'. It was the lyrical channel through which 'all the pain, all the ritual gestures of the race, can escape'.

For Lorca, the appeal of both the haiku and the copla was their power of poetic concentration. In a reaction to what he described as the 'overluxuriant lyrical tree' inherited from Romanticism, Lorca developed an appreciation for the ways in which the authors of these forms could 'condense all the highest emotional moments of life into a three- or four-line stanza'.

New Songs, a poem from Lorca's first collection, provides an insight into the aspirations he had for his poetry at this time. In the poem, Lorca longs for 'a luminous and tranquil song', 'a song to go to the soul of things', 'a song without lyrical flesh', 'a flock of blind doves tossed into mystery'.

The power of the traditional folk lyric also resonated deeply with haiku master, Matsuo Bashō. On his journey to the far north of Japan, Bashō encountered a rice planting ritual, in which the women of the remote village through which he was travelling began to sing songs as they worked; songs that, Bashō observed, had all but been forgotten throughout the rest of the country. Sensing in these songs (much as Lorca did in the songs that poured out of the Gypsy blacksmith forges of Andalusia) a purity of lyric expression, Bashō composed the following haiku:-

> the beginning of art –
> a rice planting song
> in the backcountry

Several commentators of the 1920's and 30's drew comparisons between the haiku and the copla. In an article published in *España* in 1920, the poet and critic Enrique Diez-Canedo highlighted similarities in the technical composition of short Japanese poems (the tanka as well as the haiku) and a form of flamenco song known as a *seguidilla.*

Diez-Canedo suggested that 'the alternating five- and seven-syllable verses of the seguidilla make the song of our people greatly resemble both classical genres of Japanese poetry'. In his *La Copla Andaluza* (1936) the Seville-based poet Rafael Cansinos-Asséns argued that 'the little Japanese poem called 'hai-kai' which is written on a cherry leaf... has vivified our copla, which fits nicely onto a cigarette paper'. In this essay, Cansinos-Asséns even went as far as to suggest that the efforts of contemporary Spanish poets in the field of haiku were simply 'coplas baptised with an exotic name', describing their works as 'true coplas, light and simple, with no rhetorical ballast, ready to fly away in a flock at the lightest breath of the Zephyr'.

Alongside the aesthetic and lyric potential of an individual poem, Lorca also saw in the haiku the possibilities of the poetic sequence. Haiku has its roots in the allied Japanese tradition of *renga,* in which groups of poets work collaboratively, each poet alternately contributing an individual verse, to compose a poem on a specific theme.

Lorca perceived in the poetic sequence the chance of capturing a particular phenomenon through a series of moments, vignettes, or 'etchings' – a technique relatively unexplored in Spanish poetry up until that point. In 1921 he composed the ten-poem haiku sequence, which he dedicated to his mother and sent her as a gift for her birthday.

In a letter to his brother Francisco, in which the haiku sequence was enclosed, Lorca declared that a haiku should 'deliver its emotion in two or three verses that sum up the entire emotional state'. However, professing in the same letter that 'I have a different style of hai-kai', he allowed for himself a more personal approach to the form, distinct from that he would have encountered in the translations of the Japanese masters. This 'little box of lyrical chocolates' was composed to celebrate his mother's birthday in 'the most modern and most exquisite way', with Lorca describing to his brother the poems as 'undoubtedly humoristic-lyrical and exquisitely incomprehensible for lots of people'.

Though these haiku contain many stylistic features that may seem out of place today, it is important to remember that, for Lorca, it was not the distinctive compositional techniques of the haiku poem that he sought to harness, but the power of its lyric concentration. As with his experimentation in other literary forms, such as the flamenco lyric and the Arabic ghazal, Lorca's approach to haiku composition was that of assimilation, rather than duplication. Pertinent to his philosophy on the imitation of traditional verse forms are his comments in a 1922 lecture on cante jondo, in which he declared that the 'ineffable modulations' of the copla should not be copied, as 'we can do nothing but muddy them', adding that 'only the very essence' could be drawn from these works, along with 'this or that trill for colouristic effect'. What he sought was an equivalence of the effect of a haiku poem, rather than a direct imitation of the form itself.

=Hai-Kais de Felicitación
a Mamá-

1
Sea para ti
mi corazón.
La luna sobre el agua
y el cerezo
en flor.

2
Hay una estrella
sobre tu casa
hay una estrella
¡Oh noche infinita!

3
Cuando yo era niño
ibas y venías
cuando fui mayor

ibas y venías.
Luego
saltarás de una lucero
a otro.

4
Guárdame.
Todas las rosas que puedas
en el cajón
del tueridor.

5
-Evocación-
Sean para ti
mis lagrimitas
las que lloré de niño
-Al marchar a Almería-

6.
Guárdame.
esas campanadas
del amanecer

7
Rosa clavel
y grabado de ajonjolí
sean para ti.

8.
Di a Isabelita
que quite a estos hai-kais
tu cáscara lírica.

9
En este hai-kai va
Un beso que me acabo
de cortar.

-y (O-(ritornello)
Sean para ti
mi corazón
la luna sobre el agua
y el cerezo
en flor.

The most vivid connection between Lorca's haiku and the copla is, fittingly, the image of the mother; a strong theme throughout flamenco song, owing to the closeness of the family structure within rural Gypsy communities. Throughout Lorca's haiku there is a longing for his mother, to whom he devotes both his 'heart' and his 'tears'. There is also reference to a previous physical parting, when the poet 'left for Almería' to attend school as a boy. The longing here is echoed in the following Gypsy siguiriya, the four-line verse form that embodies the most profound and emotional expression of Andalusian deep song:

> Por una ventana
> que al campo salía,
> yo daba voces a la mare de mi alma
> y no me respondía

> Through a window
> that was facing the fields,
> I was calling to the mother of my soul
> and she didn't answer me.

It is less common to find examples of such subjective longings in haiku, traditionally a more objective form of poetic expression. The discipline of the haiku poet is to offer the moment that causes him or her to feel, and not to state overtly the emotion it inspires – a successful haiku allows readers to experience the emotion for themselves. But there are more emotive examples of haiku in the work of Kobayashi Issa, whose life was beset by personal tragedy, and whose mother died when he was two years old. Throughout Issa's poetry, we feel the ache of a childhood wound:-

> mother I never knew,
> every time I see the ocean,
> every time –

In Lorca's haiku sequence, alongside imagery that abounds in traditional Japanese verse, such as 'the moon on the water', and 'the cherry tree in flower', we also encounter the natural imagery of the 'rose, carnation / and sesame seed'. In an assertion that embodies much of the sentiment of the Japanese haiku masters, Lorca once wrote that 'The poet is the medium / of Nature'. Yet, as well as evoking the glancing encounters

138

with the natural world that are so highly valued in the haiku form, we can also sense in this imagery an echo of the Gypsy lullabies and cradle songs, sung by the mothers of rural Andalusia to their babies (a form of song which Lorca would also go on to study in great detail):-

> Clavelito encarnado,
> rosa en capullo,
> duérmete, vida mía,
> mientras te arroyo.

> Little pink carnation,
> rose yet to bud,
> sleep now, my treasure,
> while I rock you.

In the verses of Issa, we find a poetry of similar maternal tenderness; a yearning for the embrace of a parent he never knew, filled with a sensitivity for the poverty of rural families:

> nursing her child
> the mother
> counts its fleabites

As well as expressing his devotion to his mother, Lorca's haiku also contain recollections of his family home; in the imagery of 'una estrella, / sobre tu casa' (a star / over your house), and in references to 'el cajón / del trinchero' (the drawer / of the carving table) in the family dining room, and to his little sister, 'Isabelita'. The family lived in Granada – a city which is 'fit for dream and daydream', which 'borders everywhere on the ineffable'. Throughout Lorca's poetry we experience Granada as more than simply a geographical setting; it is an intensely aesthetic reflection of the poet's own image and personality. A strong theme found throughout lighter forms of flamenco song is one which praises certain towns and cities, especially Granada. In one of the haiku in this sequence, Lorca implores his mother to save him 'esas campanadas / del amanecer' (those bell strokes / of dawn), reminiscent of this *media granaína,* a form of song native to the city:-

Quiero vivir en Graná
porque me gusta el oír
la campana de la Vela
cuando me voy a dormir

I want to live in Granada
because it pleases me to hear
the bell of the Vela
when I go to sleep.

There is also an echo of this lyric, and of the bell of the Vela (which is rung from a watchtower in the Alhambra to signal the opening and closing of the irrigation canals below), in Lorca's *Ghazal of the Love that Hides from Sight* from *The Tamarit Divan*:

Solamente por oír
la campana de la Vela
te puse una corona de verbena.

*Granada era una luna
ahogada entre las yedras.*

(Just to hear / the bell of the Vela / I made you a crown of verbena. *Granada was a moon / drowned in the ivy.*)

There are many examples of this longing for home in the masterpieces of traditional haiku, whose authors were very often wanderers, monks and beggars. In moments when the world of non-attachment was pierced by melancholic yearnings for home, family, lovers, or friends, we find examples of poetry such as this, from Bashō.

even in Kyoto
hearing the cuckoo's cry –
I long for Kyoto

The work of Lorca's most permeated by the haiku spirit is the *Suites* (1983). Though not published until long after his death, the wistful poems of this collection were written around the same time he produced his haiku sequence. Compared to the birthday haiku, the wistful poems

140

of *Suites* contain passages that much more closely resemble haiku as we recognise it today, suggestive of a development of compositional awareness of the form:-

> El buey
> cierra sus ojos
> lentamente...
> (Calor de establo.)

> The bullock
> slowly
> shuts his eyes.
> Heat in the stable.

> Un pájaro tan sólo
> canta.
> El aire multiplica.

> Only a single bird
> is singing.
> The air multiplies it.

> A lo lejos,
> garzas color de rosa
> y un volcán marchito

> In this distance,
> pink coloured herons
> and the spent volcano.

The poetic sequences in *Suites* are composed with a concision and structural simplicity that is true to both the tradition of the haiku and that of the 'miniature' he thought characteristic of the city of Granada. Critical to an appreciation of Lorca's haiku, and of his experimentation with the short verse form, is the aesthetic of the diminutive in the art, music and poetry of his city; a diminutive 'without rhythm, almost without grace and charm', a diminutive which 'opens secret chambers of feeling', and whose mission is to 'place in our hands objects and ideas which seem too large: time and space, the sea, the moon, distances'. For

141

it is the poetic concentration of the diminutive verse, where the lyrical tremor reaches 'a point that is inaccessible to any but a few poets', that gives so much of Lorca's early work (and the finest examples of haiku and copla) its power.

In 1932, Lorca would deliver a lecture on the *duende,* the elemental, demonic earth spirit, embodying irrationality, darkness and an awareness of death. For Lorca, the appearance of the duende in literature, art and performance was not a question of technical ability, but of 'true, living style, of blood, of the most ancient culture, of spontaneous creation'. And it is this profound authenticity which resonates in the finest examples of both the haiku and the copla. For both forms are, at their purest, 'a momentary burst of inspiration, the blush of all that is truly alive . . . the trembling of the moment and then a long silence'.

Hai-kais de felicitación de mamá

Sea para ti	May my heart
mi corazón.	be yours.
La luna sobre el agua	The moon on the water
y el cerezo en flor.	and the cherry tree in flower.

Hay una estrella,	There is a star,
sobre tu casa	over your house
hay una estrella.	there is a star.
. . . .	. . . .
¡Oh noche infinita!	Oh infinite night!

Cuando yo era niño	When I was a boy
ibas y venías.	you would come and go.
Cuando fui mayor	When I grew older
ibas y venías.	you would come and go.
. . . .	. . . .
Luego…	Some day…
saltarás de un lucero	you will leap from one star
a otro.	to another.

142

Guárdame
todas las risas que puedas
en el cajón
del trinchero.

Save me
all the laughter you can
in the drawer
of the carving table.

EVOCACIÓN

EVOCATION

Sean para ti
mis lagrimitas,
las que lloré de niño
–al marchar a Almería.

May my tears
be yours,
the ones I cried as a boy
– when I left for Almería.

Guárdame
esas campanadas
del amanecer.

Save me
those bell strokes
of dawn.

Rosa, clavel
y grano de ajonjolí
sean para ti.

These are for you:
rose, carnation
and sesame seed.

Di a Isabelita
que quite a estos *hai-kais*
su cáscara lírica.

Tell Isabelita
to remove these *hai-kais*
from their lyrical shell.

En este *hai-kai* va
un beso que me acabo
de cortar.

Enclosed in this *hai-kai*
a kiss, newly
cut

RITORNELLO

Sean para ti
mi corazón,
la luna sobre el agua
y el cerezo
en flor.

May my heart
be yours,
the moon on the water
and the cherry tree
in flower.